THE WIDOW À LA MODE

Borgo Press Books by Frank J. Morlock

Castor and Pollux and Other Opera Libretti (Editor)
The Chevalier d'Éon and Other Short Farces (Editor)
Chuzzlewit
Congreve's Comedy of Manners
Crime and Punishment
Cyrano and Molière: Five Plays by or About Molière (Editor)
Doctor Scratch and Other Plays (Editor)
Falstaff (with Shakespeare, John Dennis, & William Kendrick)
Fathers and Sons
Herculaneum & Sardanapalus: Two Opera Libretti (Editor)
The Idiot
Isle of Slaves and Other Plays (Editor)
Jurgen
Justine
The Key to the Great Gate and Other Plays
The Londoners & The Green Carnation: Two Plays
Lord Jim
Mademoiselle Fifi and Other Plays (Editor)
The Madwoman of Beresina & Other Napoleonic Plays (Editor)
Mimi Pinson and Other Plays (Editor)
Notes from the Underground
Oblomov
Old Creole Days
Outrageous Women: Lady Macbeth and Other Plays (Editor)
Parades and Proverbs: Eight Plays (Editor)
Peter and Alexis
The Princess Casamassima
A Raw Youth
The Rose Princess and Other Plays
Salammbô & Dido: Two Operas (Editor)
The Stendhal Hamlet Scenarios and Other Shakespearean Shorts from the French (Editor)
Two Voltairean Plays: The Triumvirate; Comedy at Ferney
Whitewashing Julia and Other Plays
The Widow à la Mode and Other Plays (Editor)
The Widow's Husband; and, Porthos in Search of an Outfit: Two Dumasian Comedies (Editor)
A Yiddish Hamlet and Other Plays
Zeneida & The Follies of Love & The Cat Who Changed into a Woman: Two Plays (Editor)

THE WIDOW À LA MODE

AND OTHER PLAYS

FRANK J. MORLOCK,

EDITOR

THE BORGO PRESS
MMXIII

THE WIDOW À LA MODE

Copyright © 2002, 2006, 2012, 2013 by Frank J. Morlock

FIRST EDITION

Published by Wildside Press LLC

www.wildsidebooks.com

DEDICATION

To Horvalis

CONTENTS

THE WIDOW À LA MODE, by Jean Donneau de Vise 9
CAST OF CHARACTERS. 10
THE PLAY 11
WAYWARD WENCHES, by Jean-François Regnard 68
CAST OF CHARACTERS. 69
SCENE I 70
SCENE II. 78
SCENE III 89
SCENE IV 96
SCENE V. 103
SCENE VI 107
SCENE VII. 111
SCENE VIII 116
THE ABDUCTIONS, by Michel Baron. 127
CAST OF CHARACTERS. 128

THE PLAY	129
THE SCHOOL FOR LOVERS, by Alain-René Lesage	192
CAST OF CHARACTERS	193
THE PLAY	194
ABOUT THE EDITOR	234

THE WIDOW À LA MODE
BY JEAN DONNEAU DE VISE

CAST OF CHARACTERS

MIRIS, the Widow of Cleon

ORPHISE, Her Sister

BEATRICE, Her Servant

CRISPIN, Cleon's Valet

DAME JEANNE

CLIDAMIS, Heir of Cleon

LUCILLE, a Neighbor

ALCIPE, a Businessman

DAMIS, Lover of Miris

A TAILOR

A BOY

A COMMISSARY

THE PLAY

DAME JEANNE:

Crispin, hurry up. Quick, get up. Crispin! He pays no attention. You always have to go find him. Crispin, wake up! May the Devil take you. Crispin! If he doesn't answer, I'm going to break the door down.

CRISPIN:

Who's calling me?

DAME JEANNE:

The Nurse.

CRISPIN:

It's not day yet. I'm sleeping.

DAME JEANNE:

You will be able to see very clearly when you are outside.

CRISPIN:

What are you crashing about for, old lady? And why are you bothering me? You take moonlight for daylight?

DAME JEANNE:

He's dead.

CRISPIN:

Who?

DAME JEANNE:

Mr. Cleon.

(Enter Beatrice)

BEATRICE:

Dame Jeanne,

DAME JEANNE:

I'm running.

BEATRICE:

Alas! He isn't breathing. Come quickly. Help!

DAME JEANNE:

I cannot wake him.

BEATRICE:

Come up, I tell you. I will make him get up! Oh, how this unhappiness afflicts me. I have no hope of his health. Crispin, hurry up. Mr. Cleon is worse. Crispin.

CRISPIN:

I'm coming.

BEATRICE:

He's coming and he doesn't budge.

CRISPIN:

(coming in, rubbing his eyes.) You can't see in this cursed house.

BEATRICE:

Run quickly to a doctor and don't stop.

CRISPIN:

You have some plan to hurry on his death?

BEATRICE:

You must get ready and dress in a hurry.

CRISPIN:

My poor Master, alas!

BEATRICE:

Ah, I am losing patience. Go quickly. Mr. Cleon is in extremity.

CRISPIN:

What! Is there no more hope for his life?

BEATRICE:

He's very bad.

CRISPIN:

But do you believe that he will die?

BEATRICE:

Yes, yes, if you don't get help in a hurry.

CRISPIN:

I think that Madame has a wealth of sorrow.

BEATRICE:

She takes this blow to heart. But get going.

CRISPIN:

She must fear widowhood a great deal. They say she will lose most of her wealth.

BEATRICE:

Oh, I'm furious.

CRISPIN:

But did Mr. Cleon think to make a will?

BEATRICE:

You won't go?

CRISPIN:

I'm hurrying.

BEATRICE:

Go then, quickly.

CRISPIN:

But did he leave us something?

BEATRICE:

What! Traitor! Do you want to let your master die without a doctor?

CRISPIN:

I'm on my way.

DAME JEANNE:

(reentering) Don't bother. Mr. Cleon has passed away. Just like a candle, alas, he was snuffed out.

BEATRICE:

What, the poor deceased is really dead?

CRISPIN:

(bawling) What, my master: I will never see you more?

BEATRICE:

Perhaps you're mistaken.

DAME JEANNE:

He's stone dead. I know well enough. I've been around plenty of corpses.

BEATRICE:

What—is he really dead? I am in despair. I served him as my master and I loved him as my father! Oh, when I was sleeping the other night, I dreamed this. Ah, ah, ah, ah.

CRISPIN:

Boo, boo, boo, boo.

DAME JEANNE:

Hoo, hoo, hoo, hoo.

CRISPIN:

I believe we are crying every way. Hoo, hoo, boo, boo, ah, ah.

BEATRICE:

It doesn't matter in what way we cry.

CRISPIN:

You don't think so? The dead are honored in several ways. To cry even with art irritates, these days. And the great alone are mourned in music.

BEATRICE:

The poor man.

CRISPIN:

By his death we lose both.

DAME JEANNE:

I never nursed a less irritating patient. He was always agreeable and docile. He always spoke to me in a civil way. Even when asking for the bedpan, as he did all too frequently.

CRISPIN:

It's got to be admitted he was a bon-vivant.

BEATRICE:

Good! I don't think we'll meet his like again. Boo, boo, boo, boo, boo, boo, boo! How miserable I am. Ah, ah, ah.

CRISPIN:

She's suffocating. It will be necessary to undo her stays. Her sighs are so huge they cannot pass.

BEATRICE:

Having cried for the Master, I am crying for Madame. Ah, if he had only left some children to his wife. His nephew is his only heir. It wouldn't have been so bad if he had children.

CRISPIN:

The nephew will get everything.

DAME JEANNE:

No children?

BEATRICE:

What will she do?

CRISPIN:

What can she do? She'll be treated as the Virgin widow.

BEATRICE:

She never had any ambition for that. Children were her passion.

CRISPIN:

In such a necessity one ought to do something. She should have foreseen this business. And so, without knowing it, one knows the job is done. She would have found the workers to do it.

BEATRICE:

Clidamis once had a passion for her. I believe he would gladly inherit the wife along with the money.

CRISPIN:

Between ourselves, I believe it. And I'd have sworn the master was somewhat jealous at times.

BEATRICE:

Assuredly Clidamis loves her, and I believe the master knew it.

DAME JEANNE:

You haven't yet buried your master and you're already proposing a husband for his widow.

BEATRICE:

But she's coming. How can we comfort her?

MIRIS:

(entering with her sister Orphise) Alas, my dear sister, I am inconsolable. Ah, my poor husband.

(falling into a chair)

ORPHISE:

Despair overwhelms her.

CRISPIN:

Why then all these cries when they are useless?

DAME JEANNE:

What! The good man is dead! No! I cannot believe it. He had so much care that it made me drink a lot.

ORPHISE:

Then go back upstairs. Don't leave him. You ought to care for him even after his death!

DAME JEANNE:

Madame, I believe I can without displeasing you give you some good advice. Sometimes one can laugh when one has ample reason to cry. Against all our ills the best remedy is to have wealth. Think about your situation. And that your sighs are not improving it. Without losing any more time, think how to avert trouble.

MIRIS:

What! Is this the advice you give me? You don't know

me.

ORPHISE:

Her wound is very deep.

MIRIS:

My husband being dead, nothing of this world reaches me.

DAME JEANNE:

Eh, my God! I've seen other widows besides you, who are thinking of their fortune while weeping about their spouse. I propose advice to you that you ought to take. A hundred devils! Your tears won't help you to live.

CRISPIN:

Dame Jeanne is right. What do you say, Beatrice? You can't eat off tears and moans.

DAME JEANNE:

In such a misfortune, on my oath, a widow the other day on Sunday made a test. And I was able to serve her with such good will.

ORPHISE:

Leave my sister in peace to dream of her sorrow.

CRISPIN:

She wants to put her nose in your affairs.

DAME JEANNE:

Me? Know, dear God, that nothing could make me do that. (She goes in)

MIRIS:

What shall I do?

BEATRICE:

Hey, there, there, your suffering will end. Soon you will be like everyone else.

MIRIS:

Ah! I don't feel such light cares. But go fetch Alcipe. He's a business man, and moreover, my advisor. He lives near here.

CRISPIN:

I'm running. But lighten my sorrows, Madame. You will soon be dressing us in mourning, right?

ORPHISE:

Without doubt.

CRISPIN:

Good, I am going to choose the colors.

MIRIS:

But listen, find clothes for yourself, Crispin. Send my tailor. Ah, how these thoughts add to my sorrows.

CRISPIN:

That's enough. Everything's going well. (Exit Crispin.)

MIRIS:

(getting up) Let's talk a little business. Neither the nurse or Crispin are able to shut up. That's why, in front of them, I was afraid to speak.

BEATRICE:

There. Courage, Madame.

ORPHISE:

You must pull yourself together and tell us what you're going to do.

MIRIS:

My husband's death has taken me by surprise. And, not having any children with him, by losing him, I lose all my great wealth.

BEATRICE:

That's what's troubling you.

MIRIS:

Eh!

MIRIS:

Believe me, Madame, your sorrow is just, and without blame you can give away your hand.

ORPHISE:

You ought to do it, sis.

BEATRICE:

This remedy will soften the greatest sorrow.

MIRIS:

Well, I'm resolved.

BEATRICE:

You're doing right, Madame.

MIRIS:

It really isn't contrary to the eternal love a woman owes her husband.

BEATRICE:

Ah, the good man loved your well-being more than you yourself do and he would rejoice to see you at your ease. That is, if among the dead, they are able to rejoice.

MIRIS:

Carry a service vessel filled with gold to Damis' home, our obliging neighbor. I will keep my money box, after I've taken out a good sum, as well as my diamonds. To Lucille I will commit this duty: to carry to some faithful friends some old clothing with lace.

BEATRICE:

When everything is out of the house, all your troubles will cease.

ORPHISE:

We need the night to do all this.

BEATRICE:

When everything is broken, don't think of anything except banishing the feelings that trouble your soul. For, to say the truth, your dead husband was more important to us than he was to you. When one is young, to have a husband already aged is a problem for the marriage. But let that pass. You had in the Master an inconvenient husband, of a bad temper, dirty, disgusting, emotional, jealous, bizarre, subject to a thousand ills, irritating, choleric, and avaricious.

MIRIS:

He was my husband.

ORPHISE:

He loved her tenderly. And at least at this moment, my sister must have her soul badly hurt and be plunged in misery.

BEATRICE:

According to custom, she should be very upset. I agree. And I don't suggest that her heart shouldn't be heavy today. On the contrary, to the eyes of the world she ought to show a profound sadness. What I tell you, I swear I am doing. And of all people, who cried louder than I? Soon, without thinking, you'll feel as you were. But at first, when one loses someone, the pain is hard.

MIRIS:

It always ought to be, when one loses a husband.

BEATRICE:

Hey, what! You want us to pretend with you. Cry till you're surfeited. Cry, cry, Madame. Why must we cry when we are laughing inside? Often custom and the law require us to cry when we feel like laughing.

(knocking) But someone knocks.

MIRIS:

(turning and throwing herself down) Open. Your expectations are vain. Having lost all, my death is certain. (low) It's Alcipe.

ALCIPE:

I am coming alone to speak to you, knowing quite well that time alone can console you.

BEATRICE:

(aside) I believe a rich spouse might do it as well.

MIRIS:

Alas, you know the cause of my sorrows. But, listen, sir. (Miris, Alcipe and Orphise speak low)

BEATRICE:

They talk so low. Why do dead men cause so much

trouble?

ALCIPE:

They can't help it.

MIRIS:

Ah, cruel custom. I cannot conceal my misery is mortal. I wish so much to die today. Who could live without wealth, with so much sorrow?

BEATRICE:

I'm of your opinion. Without money you cannot live.

MIRIS:

Ah, my poor husband, I'm coming to follow you.

ALCIPE:

But if his heir wishes to marry you?

MIRIS:

Hey, what! You dare to propose to me today?

ALCIPE:

What I told you ought to incline you to it.

ORPHISE:

You ought to listen to this healthy advice. And think: when fate treats you harshly, that someone beside Clidamis has a passion for you.

BEATRICE:

He has it still, if you wish, Madame. And your tearful eyes will rekindle it.

MIRIS:

Ah, don't hold such talk with me.

BEATRICE:

Oh, well, they can speak of it some other time. You are afraid of sinning against decency.

MIRIS:

But if he had only indifference for me, would you think it good that being a widow for half a day, my interest obliged me to show him love?

ORPHISE:

Only permit him to revive a dead hope, that he may still love you. But someone's knocking on the door.

MIRIS:

Open. Ha, ha, alas. How strong is my sorrow. But I mustn't hinder myself because of Crispin.

CRISPIN:

Madame, in a short time I've been everywhere and notified everyone. While sighing, I told them what had happened and they listened as if about to laugh. And they are coming here to weep with you.

BEATRICE:

Someone's at the door.

MIRIS:

(low to Alcipe) Don't open.

ALCIPE:

No. I have nothing more to say. Count on me. Take courage. Hide your papers. In a short time you will see me and I will do everything I can for you. Promise. (Alcipe leaves)

MIRIS:

Open. Leave me here. No, nothing can console me.

CRISPIN:

(opening the door) Is she prepared?

BEATRICE:

She knows very well how to play her part.

MIRIS:

Oh, my poor husband whom I lost this very day.

LUCILLE:

(entering) I come as your friend, your neighbor, because I feel for you.

MIRIS:

My unhappiness is immense, my trouble is infinite.

LUCILLE:

We all have to die; we will have our turn.

BEATRICE:

What a nasty way to console people.

LUCILLE:

He's really dead?

CRISPIN:

So much the worse.

LUCILLE:

What a loss, madam.

BEATRICE:

Does she think she's going to banish sorrow from her soul this way?

CRISPIN:

That's the way to make things worse.

BEATRICE:

That's the way it's done these days.

MIRIS:

When the poor departed was angry with me, after softening me up he didn't know what to do.

BEATRICE:

It's true. In order to appease him, often one had to carefully undress and bathe him.

LUCILLE:

He was nice when he was with women. Always laughing, always trying to kiss them. Don't cry. Oh, oh, and how your great heart throbs. Can't stop beating from sorrow. Hey, hey, hey! When crying one loses all one's charms.

BEATRICE:

Do as I do and restrain your tears. Ah, ah, ah. But I'm crying.

CRISPIN:

There's nothing to it. You laugh.

BEATRICE:

Me. I'm laughing.

CRISPIN:

Yes. You laugh the way they cry in Paris. I have a clever wit. Ah, ah, I don't know what I'm saying. And if I cry also, I cry in order to laugh. But still, my intent is to be afflicted. At this time my mouth laughed without my permission.

MIRIS:

To die so suddenly.

BEATRICE:

Being young and pretty your pain won't last forever. And you can wear out four husbands.

CRISPIN:

(aside) At least we'll have several charivaris.

LUCILLE:

Time eases the worst of sorrows.

CRISPIN:

(speaking low to Beatrice as Miris whispers to Lucille) Tell me, you who know my mistress' wealth. Will she have enough to do something for us?

BEATRICE:

Alas.

MIRIS:

Take these. (giving diamonds) Hide them so that no one will see them.

LUCILLE:

Count on me.

CRISPIN:

To cry without saying anything to me! You couldn't give me a worse answer.

MIRIS:

Ah, how I lose friends and wealth today. To whom can I confide? Who will be my support? Men are deceivers, and every day you find that the friends of the husband are not the friends of the widow. But how chagrined I'll be to see myself during my first year of mourning: all dressed in black!

ORPHISE:

Better wear a blindfold, sis.

MIRIS:

That's my trouble. For I have a strong dislike for blindfolds. What will I do with a blindfold? Oh, my poor husband!

LUCILLE:

You have a good complexion. It will become you. Goodbye. And believe, my dear, that the excess of your sorrows touches me to my very soul. (Exit Lucille)

MIRIS:

A handkerchief, Beatrice.

ORPHISE:

You haven't eaten.

BEATRICE:

I am going to go find something. (Exit Beatrice)

MIRIS:

My afflicted spirit prevents me from eating.

CRISPIN:

Her sadness is profound.

MIRIS:

After such a misfortune, I am going to quit the world.

CRISPIN:

When a woman has once been touched by a man, it isn't without reason that he is regretted. He was still speaking yesterday, my poor late master, and near as death was, he was unaware.

ORPHISE:

He could speak yesterday and die today.

CRISPIN:

I will never find another master like him.

BEATRICE:

(returning with food) Here take it. But try not to cry anymore and ruin your face in the wash. I just looked at the pot, and having found it good, I thought I should bring you some broth. You ought to try it.

MIRIS:

I don't know.

CRISPIN:

I bet she cannot do it.

MIRIS:

I don't have the courage.

ORPHISE:

But you ought to take it. It will do you good.

MIRIS:

Oh, well, give it to me. I'll do it to please you.

CRISPIN:

But I hear a knock.

MIRIS:

What shall I do?

BEATRICE:

Take it quickly.

MIRIS:

It's too hot. Take it, Crispin.

CRISPIN:

That's what I need. I haven't eaten!

ORPHISE:

See at the door.

CRISPIN:

It's necessary in taking it to show a strong character.

BEATRICE:

(having opened, hears a voice)

VOICE:

How is Mr. Cleon since yesterday?

BEATRICE:

He's dead.

VOICE:

That's fine.

CRISPIN:

My word, he was good. But he gave me a hard time.

BEATRICE:

Take your broth without waiting any more.

MIRIS:

Give it here.

CRISPIN:

What? I just ate it like you told me.

MIRIS:

You were supposed to hide it.

CRISPIN:

I thought I was supposed to drink it down in a hurry.

BEATRICE:

If—

MIRIS:

Take care what you say. In the mood I am in, don't make me laugh.

BEATRICE:

Then take this biscuit which I took for myself. You ought to eat it.

MIRIS:

Oh, for God's sake, shut up.

ORPHISE:

But take it, sis. I'm the one who's asking you. You have to eat a bit to conserve your strength.

MIRIS:

Oh well, give it to me. I have no appetite. (she devours the biscuit)

CRISPIN:

Look at that after all her scorn.

BEATRICE:

Instead of afflicting yourself, think that widowhood has its pleasures just like marriage. No longer disturbed, you will henceforth see the world at your liberty.

MIRIS:

Ah, my poor husband. (chewing the biscuit.)

BEATRICE:

That's not him, Miris, it's a muffin.

ORPHISE:

Her pain pierces her to the soul.

CRISPIN:

Plague. How fast she eats. It's almost gone.

ORPHISE:

Her pain pierces my heart.

BEATRICE:

She eats with fury because she's afflicted.

MIRIS:

I'm full.

CRISPIN:

That's easy to believe. When you eat that fast, you have to have a drink.

ORPHISE:

Won't you have something to drink, sis. How'd you like some wine?

MIRIS:

Yuck!

ORPHISE:

It will refresh your spirit. (knocking)

MIRIS:

Now who is it? If they learn I'm eating, a hundred busy

bodies will find it strange, and say that I shouldn't do it no matter how you urge me.

CRISPIN:

(opening the door) The day a husband dies, nobody eats or drinks.

BEATRICE:

As for me, I find that custom strange.

MIRIS:

Oh, don't talk about it.

ORPHISE:

Why, it's Mr. Damis.

DAMIS:

(entering) Having always vowed to be your friend, I ask you to witness how much I share in your sorrows.

CRISPIN:

I am greatly obliged to have you console the afflicted. If your wife died, people would do the same for you.

MIRIS:

I wish that my extreme sorrow allowed me to give a better response to your kindness.

DAMIS:

Robust and healthy, I don't know how death took him in only four days. I think I still see him in his chamber walking with his nightcap.

CRISPIN:

That would be a white one. The one he wore yesterday was a yellow one.

BEATRICE:

Alas.

DAMIS:

Console yourself.

MIRIS:

Ah, if I lose my husband, time can never ease my pain. When something was bothering the poor man, he'd tell me about it all night.

BEATRICE:

What, Madame, do you complain only about this subject? If the poor man hadn't done it, there'd be nothing much to complain of.

MIRIS:

He had a good soul.

ORPHISE:

One cannot find a better person.

DAMIS:

I believe that one cannot even mourn him enough.

BEATRICE:

All men are good when they are dead.

DAMIS:

Let us go. In sorrow, everybody's a nuisance. (Exit Damis)

CRISPIN:

To leave this way is to leave fashionably.

MIRIS:

Now I can breathe a minute.

BEATRICE:

Yes, if you wish it.

ORPHISE:

Go up quickly to hide your papers.

MIRIS:

If someone asks for me, say that I cannot be seen.

ORPHISE:

Go on, I know what to do. Again, something irritating. (Exit Miris)

CRISPIN:

Despite his faults, she still really loves him.

BEATRICE:

He caused her sighs.

CRISPIN:

Someone's coming.

(Enter Clidamis)

BEATRICE:

It's Clidamis.

CRISPIN:

I believe he laughs in his soul.

BEATRICE:

Sir, right now one cannot see Madame.

CRISPIN:

If the poor departed had left a will— But, alas, he died so suddenly.

CLIDAMIS:

I take pity of the sorrows which heaven sends you.

CRISPIN:

Heirs like you who find money to count never cry from joy. They've not the time to feel sad.

BEATRICE:

With wealth can one feel sorrow?

CLIDAMIS:

All that I have is for your mistress.

BEATRICE:

Crispin, go put on your clothes.

CRISPIN:

I will return in a moment! (Exit Crispin)

BEATRICE:

To hear you talk, one would say your soul retains the ardor of its first flame.

CLIDAMIS:

I swear that I loved your mistress before marriage took her under its laws. But what do I say? I feel that my heart still loves her. And to tell you more, that I feel I adore her. But the time is unsuitable to reveal my passion, and I cannot hope to obtain recognition.

BEATRICE:

I intend to be a big help to you if you second me.

CLIDAMIS:

Tell me what can be done.

BEATRICE:

Show her that all the wealth of her departed spouse belongs to you according to law. For that, I think it will be necessary to apply promptly to the courts and have a magistrate appointed.

CLIDAMIS:

That would insult her. I don't agree with you. I ought to spare her such a charming sight.

BEATRICE:

From decency she must feel she is forced to suffer the ardor of the passion your soul is full of. That way she can meet the criticism of the self-appointed censors who criticize morals. Leave the rest to me.

CLIDAMIS:

Give me your word.

BEATRICE:

Go. I promise you to play my role well. Don't waste time. (Exit Clidamis) So. My way, she'll save all her wealth.

CRISPIN:

(entering with tailor and used-clothes dealer) Here's

your tailor and used-clothes dealer.

DEALER:

I've come to find you as you told me. And I haven't forgotten your mourning. Take it. I'm sure it's made for you.

TAILOR:

(measuring) There.

BEATRICE:

Very good.

CRISPIN:

I'm in a hurry and I've a lot to do.

DEALER:

You already tried the doublet and the pants at my shop.

CRISPIN:

Right.

DEALER:

You won't find anything better. But let's look at the coat.

CRISPIN:

We'll see.

BEATRICE:

This is good, too.

TAILOR:

(to Beatrice who's on a ladder) But why are you perching thus?

CRISPIN:

I'm dreaming and I don't understand anything.

BEATRICE:

It shouldn't be hard to understand. I intend that you take my measurements while I'm on this ladder. I want a long train.

CRISPIN:

You'll have to appease her.

TAILOR:

I'll satisfy her if she'll let me do it.

DEALER:

(low to Crispin) She intends to prevent any theft.

TAILOR:

Do you know I can hear you talking?

BEATRICE:

That's too small.

TAILOR:

But Madam will be enraged, and I want to talk to her before doing anything.

DEALER:

It's practically new.

CRISPIN:

I'm afraid it's not new.

DEALER:

It's completely new, I tell you, and it's apparent to anyone. Jumps right out at you.

BEATRICE:

Kindly don't steal when you make my dress.

DEALER:

You accuse him wrongly; he never steals.

TAILOR:

They know ragmen.

DEALER:

They know tailors.

CRISPIN:

I don't know which of the two is the better.

TAILOR:

Goodbye. Kindly let me know what I should do about your train. (Exit Tailor)

BEATRICE:

There. Let's see this outfit.

CRISPIN:

I've already bought them from him.

BEATRICE:

You say this outfit has never been worn?

DEALER:

I'm selling it as is. But I bet only a brand new one could serve him better.

CRISPIN:

If you wish to have it, it would delight me.

DEALER:

As I hope to have the honor to serve you, I will make it cheap. Without wasting time in useless words, give me three crowns.

BEATRICE:

Well, without bargaining, I'll give you half that.

DEALER:

I would give you more from friendship.

BEATRICE:

Well, I'd give you only half a crown more.

CRISPIN:

(looking at her pitifully) Beatrice.

BEATRICE:

That's enough. I give my word. Madame would criticize me if I gave too much.

DEALER:

I lose. But I'll chalk it up to experience.

BEATRICE:

Here. (giving money)

DEALER:

And the boy gets nothing?

BEATRICE:

Here again.

DEALER:

Goodbye. You are an honest woman. (Exit Old-Clothes Dealer)

BEATRICE:

Alas, my poor master.

CRISPIN:

By the way, he is dead.

BEATRICE:

I can see that your clothes rejoice you so much you are thinking no more of it.

CRISPIN:

I forgot my sorrow. But I believe I hear my mistress coming down. (Enter Miris and Orphise)

CRISPIN:

I've got my lace mourning. Beatrice paid for it.

MIRIS:

He tried it on first, I hope.

BEATRICE:

Yes.

ORPHISE:

How much did it cost?

CRISPIN:

(low to Beatrice) Are we going to jack it up?

BEATRICE:

It cost me five crowns.

CRISPIN:

She's very credulous. They easily deceived her.

BEATRICE:

I saw your tailor, and said that for your honor you wished to make me a long train for my dress.

CRISPIN:

She's the one who doesn't want the tailor to rob her.

BEATRICE:

He's a very honest man. He told me a hundred times he wouldn't ever take four for a fabric.

CRISPIN:

No, because he couldn't take more.

(Enter a Court Officer/Commissaire/Bailiff)

CRISPIN:

But what do I see, Madame? This is a man who frightens women, who worsens the pain in the homes of the departed, and who, often enough, widows greatly fear. A Bailiff who takes bad measures.

BEATRICE:

Then you come here to seal our locks?

CRISPIN:

We say nothing to you of the wealth which is here. And now it is necessary to seal we will conceal. And we will do a lot without applying wax.

BAILIFF:

I excuse your sorrow and wish to leave you to your grief. But I have a writ from Clidamis to seal and inventory.

ORPHISE:

Go up with him, Crispin. (Exit Bailiff and Crispin)

MIRIS:

Oh, god, how upset I am. See, see now, how Clidamis loves me.

BEATRICE:

Perhaps it's nothing but a stratagem which he believes will force you to see him. He's trying to demonstrate to you in a small way how much power he has.

ORPHISE:

If Beatrice is right, relax. You will gain 2,000 crowns income by this.

MIRIS:

From what you tell me, he doesn't love me. Wealth charms him more than my weak attractions.

DAME JEANNE:

(entering) Mercy God. You know, Mr. Bailiff, that I fear nothing.

ORPHISE:

Why don't you shut up?

DAME JEANNE:

Me, shut up? No, no. I will not shut up. No one can outrage Dame Jeanne to this point. I will make you see that I have courage.

MIRIS:

But what's wrong with you?

ORPHISE:

Then tell us what outrage happened?

DAME JEANNE:

I'm not going to leave without speaking. I want to give him reason. I haven't lived to let somebody surprise me. And he doesn't know his business, but he's going to learn it.

ORPHISE:

But tell us: what is all this rage about?

DAME JEANNE:

It suffices, as they say, that his isn't much.

MIRIS:

Don't make so much trouble. I don't want anything to do with this business. And you would put me in trouble with the Bailiff.

DAME JEANNE:

He's a bad counselor who ought to know my rights. And who separates me according to his laws. By God, I intend that he do me justice. But as you wish me to explain to you: know that he wants to seal that which I ought to have. If he knew his job properly, he would know that he shouldn't touch certain clothes that the deceased often give their nurses.

MIRIS:

Don't bother me any more about this. Rely on me. You won't need to complain. I'll get what's yours.

BEATRICE:

Madam, it isn't time to make a mystery of the love that Clidamis has for you but doesn't know how to express. He told me—me, myself, today. You can have the wealth he has for little more than giving his love the right to hope.

ORPHISE:

Sis, in conscience think that you ought to consider your benefit.

BEATRICE:

Can you do better?

ORPHISE:

Everywhere they say he's a fine man. And, having already known how to please him, you ought to love him. Do it before the Bailiff leaves.

MIRIS:

Yes. What will people say?

BEATRICE:

Oh. What people will say is not a consideration. And far from thinking of it, consider, Madam, that when sorrow leaves you—for in time that's a certainty—you'll want to laugh often after having wept. Now, that's impossible when one is too poor. Despite yourself, you'll always be weeping.

MIRIS:

My husband only died today. This effort—

BEATRICE:

Well, after some time he will be very long dead. From generosity your lover will turn furious and will allow you to weep a while longer from policy. There he is. (to Clidamis) You ought to speak to her without delay. Madam by me wishes to know your love.

CLIDAMIS:

Very good. My sad heart sighs for her attractions. I wouldn't have spoken of it to her so soon.

(to Miris) Madam, as yet I dare not speak to you of the pressing ardor with which I feel myself burning. When you have so many sorrows of the soul, it is not time to speak of a passion.

ORPHISE:

Answer.

MIRIS:

I cannot.

BEATRICE:

You ought.

MIRIS:

Leave me.

BEATRICE:

But you ought to say something.

MIRIS:

Oh, please shut up.

CLIDAMIS:

I see with what emotion you suffer my presence.

BEATRICE:

At least say something that will give him some hope.

MIRIS:

Sir, you know very well that, my husband having died today, I cannot. But when I think of you, I am not thinking of what I am going to do. And for a while at least, my heart must be silent.

ORPHISE:

What you tell him nothing?

MIRIS:

Oh, God, what a situation.

BEATRICE:

But do you hate him?

MIRIS:

Me, hate him? Alas —

BEATRICE:

What do you mean to say with that "alas"?

ORPHISE:

From love and sorrow her aching heart sighs.

BEATRICE:

I think that "alas" is a sign of tenderness for you. And you will see that she will speak for you. This is all she can do at present, and I think that's all she needs to say as a new widow.

CLIDAMIS:

This language of the heart. This obliging "alas." Does it announce my happiness?

BEATRICE:

Ah! Don't press her. Silence is consent. It should suffice for that she only sighs without rejecting your love.

CLIDAMIS:

What don't I owe you!

MIRIS:

I've said too much. Goodbye. (Exit Miris.)

BEATRICE:

This was a plain answer to your flame. You see what my work has done for you?

DAME JEANNE:

Make the Bailiff leave promptly.

CLIDAMIS:

That's my intent.

ORPHISE:

So much the better.

BEATRICE:

(to audience) You see plainly that we've all been made to laugh from all this weeping.

CURTAIN

WAYWARD WENCHES
BY JEAN-FRANÇOIS REGNARD

CAST OF CHARACTERS

Mezzetin, also Croquignolet, and as a Dutchman

Pierrot

Columbine

Harlequin, also as Commissar

Isabelle, also Glandine

Cinthio

Pasquariel

Five men, two women

SCENE I

Mezzetin

What do I see, Pierrot? Am I having hallucinations? Yes? No? It's she, it's my sister!

Pierrot

Your sister? I don't believe it without touching her, sir.

Mezzetin

It's herself—and what are you doing here, Miss Runaway?

Columbine

Oh, brother dear, don't get upset. I will tell you.

Mezzetin

And what will you tell me, brazen one? Wait—it makes me want to make a mess of your gizzard.

Columbine

My poor Pierrot.

Pierrot

My poor Pierrot! Your brother's right. As for me, I love honor, and I don't like it for a girl to frequent night haunts.

Mezzetin

Speak then, tell me what reason you had to leave the paternal house?

Pierrot

Sir, do you want to bet that it's love that's taken the field? Girls are ships that ordinarily don't sail forth, except in that wind.

Columbine

I will tell you, brother, that as soon as you had left, there came a young knight—the politest knight in the world, to ask for a room in our hotel. To not appear less polite than he, I made all the courtesies of which I was capable. So why did you leave me alone? (she says this in tears)

Pierrot

I have always told you, sir, company is necessary for girls—be it only a broomstick.

Mezzetin

Well, then?

Columbine

As soon as he arrived, he begged me, but in the most polite way in the world, to give him a room. So to please him, from politeness, I showed him the best room in the house myself: the one at the foot of the courtyard.

Pierrot

From politeness?

Columbine

From politeness. But he didn't want to stay there, fearing it would not be healthy because of the humidity.

Mezzetin

He was right.

Columbine

Seeing that he had difficulty in staying in that room—

and that he was so polite—I took him to another room which gave on the street—over the stable.

Pierrot

From politeness?

Columbine

From politeness. But he proved to me he couldn't sleep there because, being tired and in need of quiet, the horses would interrupt his sleep at night.

Mezzetin

Listen, there's a fellow who has a lot of trouble getting sleep.

Pierrot

Perhaps, not so much as you think.

Columbine

I found his thinking was good—for when one is trying to sleep, it's irritating to be interrupted. Seeing that he needed rest and that he always displayed the most polite manners, I felt obliged to put him in a place far away from any noise. You know that my room gives on the garden, and I took him there.

Pierrot

From politeness?

Columbine

Assuredly. Wouldn't you have done that in my place, Pierrot?

Pierrot

Without doubt! And, I would be furious if someone else were more polite than I was.

Mezzetin

There's politeness that could indeed lead us into crime.

Columbine

He found that my room was good enough for him, and made me understand that he would be delighted to sleep there. I told him as well, that since this spot pleased him, I would put a bed for him beside mine.

Pierrot

From politeness?

Columbine

What do you think? But, as he was extremely polite, he

refused the offer which I made him for fear of inconveniencing me, and said that he wouldn't suffer that my room be disturbed for love of him, and that he would sooner sleep in the stable than cause me the least inconvenience.

Pierrot

Oh, in a stable—the poor young man. That makes me pity him.

Columbine

His politeness broke my heart. A girl isn't made of wood, and seeing that my room pleased him so much, I told him—but you will get angry?

Mezzetin

No, no.

Columbine

I told him—but, promise me you won't be furious?

Pierrot

Ouf—watch out for politeness!

Columbine

I told him he could sleep in my bed.

Pierrot

From politeness. My word, sir, you have a well-schooled sister.

Mezzetin

Oh, sister knows how to live. It's not a great misfortune. You went to sleep in another room?

Columbine

I could have, of course, but I was not in control. He would never let me inconvenience myself for love of him. He said he was in despair to have despoiled me of my bed, and—

Pierrot

Now, that's a polite fellow.

Mezzetin

All right, then, what are you trying to say?

Columbine

He said he'd loved me for a long while, and that he wished to be my husband, and he gave me his promise, which I still have—

Mezzetin

Ah, unfortunate girl. So, that's it, just heaven. But you won't escape my vengeance, and—

Pierrot

Never mind, sir, a good marriage will settle everything.

Columbine

I don't see how it was such a bad thing to sleep with one's husband.

Mezzetin

It is necessary to try to remedy all this. Enter into this hostel, and take care to say that you know me.

Pierrot

My word, I keep coming back to it. Here's a polite girl, to give half of her bed to a lad—and then, the poor child, the poor child.

CURTAIN

SCENE II

Harlequin without his mask, holding a knapsack on his shoulder. Mezzetin as Croquignolet. Isabelle as Glandine, servant of the inn.

Harlequin

Damn, sir! I am unable to go any further. I have a raw ass! Plague on all trips. Did they send you a summons, and are you going to see the army?

Mezzetin

It's that I have a martial heart.

Harlequin

I believe that. Mr. Croquignolet, your father, and Madame Croquignolet, your mother, will be very surprised when we arrive in their shop to see their son, the lawyer, returning from Flanders.

Mezzetin

Oh, I believe it.

Harlequin

All the strollers in the quarter will crowd into your shop, to know the news of the war.

Mezzetin

That'll be funny enough—to a young practitioner like me, to have already seen a tumultuous battle, and to be returned safe and sound.

Harlequin

Oh, by God, sir, you can go anywhere, like this—and I guarantee you will never be injured.

Mezzetin

It's still a little hot.

Harlequin

True, but you took the air on Mount Pagnote at three long leagues from the cannon.

Mezzetin

I didn't go to get myself stupidly killed. It wouldn't have been honest for me to die of it, and I would've been enraged for the rest of my life, if I wasn't killed like a fool.

Harlequin

Ho! You're right, sir. Let's get to the country, if you please. Let us go quickly to your father, to visit his Burgundy wine, for I feel the need of strength.

Mezzetin

Ho, I am warned against going to my father.

Harlequin

And, by whom?

Mezzetin

They sent to tell me at the army, that my big sister, Toinon, had the smallpox, and I wouldn't enjoy being scarred by it.

Harlequin

It's much better to protect your complexion, and it will be really insulting for a young man who has been spared by the cannon to expose himself to such an insolent malady. Let's stop at the first hostel—I believe this one will do our business.

(Harlequin knocks at the door of the Inn.)

Isabelle (under the name of Glandine, servant of the Inn)

Good day, gentlemen. What do you wish?

Harlequin

Come, child, a room, a fire, and a good meal. I will stop willingly enough where there's good wine and a pretty wench.

Isabelle

Gentlemen, you will have everything you want. We lack nothing here.

Mezzetin

Come, child, take off my boots. (he raises his foot for Isabelle)

Isabelle (pushing him off)

Take your boots off? Sir, go find your girls to do that. It's not my business.

Mezzetin

You mean you're not also the valet of this stable?

Harlequin

Sir, there's a wench that seems very determined, but it seems to me she's raking you over the coals a little.

Mezzetin

My word, this little baggage is pretty. Come here, child. Are you married?

Isabelle

No, sir, thank God. I have no such honor. It is a bad year for girls. All the boys are gone to war.

Harlequin

And still there is one who isn't. If this little baggage wanted to, we'd soon bring this affair to its conclusion.

Mezzetin

I feel that something is tickling me. Hey, do you quite understand me?

Isabelle (shrugging her shoulders)

Here's a real imbecile.

Harlequin (to Isabelle, low)

It's a dummy with no common sense.

Mezzetin (making leering faces at Isabelle)

If you wanted me to relax from my martial exploits—I have some money, yes.

Isabelle

Good, I'm quite safe with your money, it's never been that that tempted me. I prefer a man who pleases me to all the treasures of the world, and if you want me to speak frankly, I prefer your valet to you. (she pushes Harlequin in the stomach)

Harlequin

On my oath, the little wench has good taste. Withdraw, sir, there aren't any secrets here for your hungry ears.

(pushing Mezzetin)

Mezzetin (coming close to Isabelle)

Do you know, little rogue, that I come from the army?

Isabelle

You from the army? You so quaintly dressed with your black clothes; it was you, then, who carried orders for the Dutch who were killed?

Mezzetin

What the devil?—if someone cared to doubt it, I could make him see that it was Mathurin Croquignolet, volunteer foot soldier, following the army.

Harlequin

And a lawyer in parliament!

Isabelle

Oh, you are a valorous person. I believe nothing could make a Mathurin Croquignolet flee from the chickens in the cellar.

Mezzetin

This baggage is not taken with my merit. I am still a scamp with the ladies. (he teases her)

Isabelle

I beg you, sir, control yourself. I don't like to be pestered. If you want to stay with us—there is the open door. If not, I am your very humble servant. (she tries to go back into the inn)

Mezzetin (holding her by the arm)

I don't wish to leave here, the pretty tavern. (he tries to enter the inn after her)

Cinthio (who has seen Mezzetin, leaves the Inn and pushes Mezzetin rudely)

By what right, sir, if you please, do you take liberties with this girl here?

Mezzetin

By what right? My right, if you please.

Cinthio

It's your pleasure? Believe me, my little drunken fool. Don't burn my ears, for I can take offense to such a thing, and it will much displease you.

Mezzetin

Sir, one doesn't treat a Parisian gentleman who's just returned from Flanders like that.

Cinthio

You, from Flanders?

Harlequin (who was hiding in a corner from fear, approaches)

May the devil carry me off if we are not come from the camp of Flanders.

Cinthio (pointing to Mezzetin)

This fellow here?

Mezzetin (swaggering)

Oh no, if I wasn't there when our general signified a hearing for our enemies—they didn't join issue after the last of July at a set hour, to plead on the field of battle—oh no, no, we weren't there.

Cinthio

Oh, oh. Here's a totally new way of fighting.

Mezzetin

The case was called; it lasted more than five hours, but because of the good cannons of which we were the carriers, we soon evicted the enemy. He wanted two or three times to plead again, but was always routed and condemned to all the expenses, damages, and interests—and costs. And, we were there? No, no, I am only joking.

Cinthio

This, I admit, is a pleasant story of combat. I quite see, sir, that you witnessed the battle as a judge advocate.

Harlequin

I am going to tell this better than my master, for between us, he's a stupid lump. First of all—there's the enemy—and there we are. Combat started with dawn. At once we were sending forward our sutters. The enemy, seeing this, detached five squadrons of their best scouts. Ha, it was there that we waited for them, for soon they launched all their galleys to break a half moon; after that musket fire, bam, bang—ha, I'm dead. The foreships, the cannon—the trumpets—were loaded with powder—bam—bully—I cannot tell the rest, for the smoke of the cannon prevented me from seeing it.

Cinthio

That's the prettiest story in the world. But, I beg you, Mr. Sutter, and you, my little paralegal, to be on your way, and not to look behind you.—understand me?

Mezzetin (becoming courageous)

Sir, take care what you do. If you insult me—

(Mezzetin takes his sword and raises it. Cinthio puts his hand on his sword.)

Cinthio

Well?

Mezzetin

You will have to deal with—(hiding behind Harlequin)—my valet.

Harlequin

Oh, my oath, he would rather kill you. I am not obliged to be killed in your place.

Cinthio

Go, my little friend. I don't deign to reply to you—but if you dare so much as to cast eyes on that girl, I will beat you to death with a stick. (he gives him a punch in the nose and leaves)

Mezzetin (after Cinthio has left)

Is he gone yet? Hey, what did I tell you? I did a job on him.

Harlequin

Ho, very good, sir. That's what comes from having been in the army.

(They go into the hotel.)

CURTAIN

SCENE III

Scene of the Fowl.

To understand this scene, it is necessary to know that Isabelle is a girl, who, having been abused by Cinthio, followed him everywhere; an indignity caused her to change her name and take service in Harlequin's hotel. She meets her betrayer with whom, in the presence of the host, this equivocal scene takes place.

Isabelle, under the name of Glandine, pushes Cinthio out the door. Harlequin has followed the noise.

Isabelle

Well, faithless one, do you recognize me now? The one you have betrayed, who was forced by you to leave her country, to find you, to reproach you with your inconstancy, disguised under the dress of a servant?

Cinthio

I tell you once more that I don't know you. Isabelle is not capable of such transport of anger, nor of throwing herself at people's heads, at all comers, as I have recently seen you do. You mock me.

Harlequin (who comes to see what all the noise is)

What the devil kind of hullabaloo is this? One would think that the devil carried off the house. It seems to me, sir, that you squeeze near my servant closely. You think one is obliged to present you with the hotel girls? My word, you'd better guard your nose.

Cinthio

Oh, oh. Here's a host quite grim. I see, indeed, that this base fellow doesn't talk nice, except to his horse. Sir, it's a little difference I had with Glandine. I asked her for a utensil of which I have need.

Harlequin

What, sir? For what do you take my wench? I beg you to understand that she is not a utensil, you hear?

Cinthio

Without so much fuss, sir, give me my bill. When you wish to keep an inn, take care to get wenches for servants who consider men of quality and treat them properly.

Harlequin

What then, rascal, what have you done that the gentleman complains of you? Haven't I told you that a serving wench must be sweet and forthcoming to the guests?

Cinthio

Hey, sir, she isn't forthcoming or sweet at all.

Harlequin

Why isn't she? This isn't the first time I've had my doubts. You see how bold the baggage is! I didn't take her to serve in the kitchen, but I quite see she belongs there.

Isabelle

If I am bold, it's not at your expense. Do you wish me to leave quite naked?

Harlequin

Yes, I wish it. A girl who doesn't earn money is born only to make beds in a hotel.

Isabelle (aside)

I've got to get out of this. (aloud) And what have I done to cause this fuss? This nice gentleman is very pleasant, to get all the girls in our hotel to serve him, and to take all our profits.

Harlequin

What then, is it only a little dirty talk on his part?

Isabelle

He said this is his sister. Hey, yes—here's a nice relative. There's never a male guest in this hotel of whom I can't be the sister—if I wanted to take the trouble. Ho, indeed, sir, I don't intend to suffer another woman take my place.

Harlequin

Glandine's right, sir. When there's a servant in a hotel, one ought to be served only by her. And besides, Glandine is very clever, which means, she makes a bed as well as a stew.

Cinthio

I know, sir, that she knows her work perfectly well. But she's a little impudent who serves at call, when she ought to serve me alone. Have I not the right to complain?

Harlequin

Assuredly, she's wrong. I will tell you now, sir, that

here everything is very exact: to give company what they ask. At this time, I don't wish to give to the stage coach a cat or a wild rabbit that the messenger had kept. Why, then, slut, have you been so impudent?

Isabelle

I—serve to another what I promised you? Say often, sir, that you, haven't wished to content yourself with what you have chosen yourself, and that an appetite has come to you while eating?

Harlequin

By God, sir, if you are fantastic, there's no way to content you.

Isabelle

You see, I beg you, if it is not enough of a meal for a man alone. I presented him with a young chicken, tender, fat right down to its nails, like me. The gentleman was not content—he still wanted another.

Harlequin

Devil, sir, if you're like that, you'd put an entire spit in your mouth at one time.

Cinthio

Oh, don't believe her. I was very pleased with the

chicken. I am not so gluttonous an eater, but I know that you present that chicken to all comers. It's already served twenty different tables, and I am not a man to share with the rest of the earth.

Harlequin

Ah, by God, sir, take care, if you please. What do you say? I cannot listen to you messing around like that, and one only serves fresh food in my hotel. Speak, has one ever eaten the same chicken twice here?

Isabelle

Indeed! Don't you see that the gentleman doesn't know what he's saying? Nobody ever touched it. It was a delicate bird that I had taken pains to raise, and that I nourished for the spit with as much pleasure as if it had been for me myself. Everyone who saw her wished to eat her and now, I kept her only for this gentleman. It's quite rude to take such little notice of the care I took for you. Perhaps you don't like meat with bacon because it makes you fat?

Cinthio

Bacon, schmacon, I don't care; when things are good, I find them so. I don't let myself be tricked.

Isabelle

To satisfy this gentleman's taste one would have to

serve him an old tough bird, some ancient of the lower court. That's how to get into his graces.

Harlequin

Oh, by God sir, if you love tough meat, we will give you all you can eat.

Cinthio

Eh, sir!

Harlequin

I have a goose that has made my soup for three months. You will have that. There isn't a stable boy bold enough to put his teeth on it.

Isabelle

That's exactly what the gentleman needs.

Harlequin

Come on, quiet down. I do not want to hear you breathe. Go back down. I quite see that the gentleman doesn't know a wench from a chicken. I'll put a side of beef on the grill for you.

CURTAIN

SCENE IV

On French morals and the manner of making love.

Columbine

Nothing is more true than what I tell you: this gentleman called Cinthio, who loves you, who swears an eternal love for you, has said as much to me, and without knowing that you give him to me because of his infidelity. I don't know if, in the end, he wouldn't succeed in breaking my heart a little.

Isabelle

Is it possible, miss, that so much love is followed by so much perfidy? No, I would never have believed that men are faithless to such a degree.

Columbine

Men—are the most cursed—! I know only one secret: so as not to be deceived, it's to deceive them first.

Isabelle

The perfidious one! After having engaged his heart to me with a promise of marriage.

Columbine

Promise of marriage! Ah! I would never believe it. A trap for dupes, a trap for dupes.

Isabelle

He had to leave me for a duel after he killed his enemy; love made me fly after his footsteps. I came to Paris, I disguised myself as a serving wench under the name Glandine. I came as a lodger in this hotel where I live—I saw him with pleasure again.— I ought to forget him forever. But, alas! When one has a sincere heart, and is not born a criminal, the way's hard.

Columbine

Oh, you must become one, otherwise, one can do nothing in love; and the virtue most needed, in this century in which we live, is a little inconstancy— seasoned sometimes with perfidy.

Isabelle

Why then, miss, with all your experience, did you let yourself be taken in like a novice? For it seems to me from your story that you were somewhat maltreated.

Columbine

I admit that I didn't get any better bargain than you. But I know what I know and, with time, I'll be wiser.

Isabelle

That means, miss, that you don't pretend to stay there, and that you don't wish to be an adventuress?

Columbine

I left home like you to follow a faithless lover I called Octavio. Cinthio came directly to take part under my standards, and if he had not acquainted me that he was a deserter by profession, I don't know if I might not have enrolled him. Dammit, in time of war, one takes what one can find.

Isabelle

What a joy, miss, to be able to change lovers so easily. And I would be content if I could only avenge myself on the infidel. I would like to be able to hate him as much as he deserves.

Columbine

Don't trouble yourself about vengeance. Only place your interest in the hands of a coquette of this country of whom he will become amorous. I promise you, she'll do him up.

Isabelle

No, no, I can't believe myself avenged by giving him to another. If a woman loves him once, she'll love him forever. And besides, French women would never let him go.

Columbine

Oh, take care. Don't you know that Paris is the boutique of lightness? A stranger never comes here without taking his position. Indeed, I tell you, it is the department store of inconstancy which provides for all Europe.

Isabelle

Is it possible? I wouldn't have believed it. Alas, when a Frenchie tells you he loves you, he says it in a manner so tender and passionate that it seems his love ought to last more than twenty years after his death.

Columbine

Twenty years after his death; my, yes—women would be happy if their love lasted only twenty days.

Isabelle

You surprise me.

Columbine

Doesn't the variety of their fashions express the inconstancy of their humor? Today they wear wigs that hang to their knees—tomorrow they wear others that don't go below their ears. They are dressed the most simply in the world; two days later, you find them in their lace and ribbons: soon they are trussed in their clothes and swaddled like mummies—and sometimes a ream of cloth wouldn't suffice to make an arm of their suits. Then all is changed, wheeling about in a Frenchie from head to foot.

Isabelle

Perhaps that's true, for adapting and the manner of dressing. But as to the heart, I can not believe it is so subject to change.

Columbine

Oh, you're right. They are mirrors of fidelity. Do you want me to describe a Frenchie who wants to awaken the tenderest heart of a young woman? First, I warn you that hot ashes are not more hot. Ah, my dear child, my princess, how many beauties, how many charms! Have the gods ever made anything so perfect as you? No, my love cannot go so far, and I am in despair at having only ordinary words to express that love: would you like me to die at your feet? You say nothing? Then I must die, because your cruelty orders it. Then he cries, he lets a burning sigh escape, he rests his head on a corner of the fireplace. Nothing more is necessary. There's a woman in the net.

Isabelle

But truly, I quite believe him. And a man who explains himself so lovingly is very lovable. Is there a way to resist such sighs? I admit it wasn't necessary to court me in such a high-falutin' style to seduce me. I feel I have a French heart.

Columbine

That's the prettiest thing in the world. But observe the reverse of the coin. I am going to make you see a Frenchie after his passion cools. That is to say, eight hours after declaring himself.

Isabelle

Let's see them.

Columbine (passing to the other side, counterfeiting a lover)

My word, Madame, I am surprised at your manners. I never come to you without having some subject of annoyance.— You come so little, monsieur, at least not so often.— By God, Madame, one has one's business.— When you started to love me, you had no other business besides love. Is this the fondness you have sworn for me?— But, Madame, that cannot always last.— But, you have taken so many oaths to me that your passion would be eternal.— Madame, I believed it. Ingrate, infidel.— Oh, Madame, no insults, you can put a placard on your door, to take lease of your heart if you care to.— There's my Frenchie gone.

Isabelle

But truly, miss, if this is true, as you wish me to believe, a Frenchie is practically no better for a woman than an Italian.

Columbine

Much worse. Believe me, from one woman to another, as a faithless one, I much prefer Octavio to any other. Goodbye, miss. I promise you that I will not spring any trap on the heart of your lover—and because of my care for you, you will have no reason to cry thief.

Isabelle

A heart is still a petty theft of which women today are not very scrupulous.

CURTAIN

SCENE V

Scene of remonstrances of Pierrot.

Harlequin

Look here, Pierrot. I am going on an important expedition. I leave you master in my place. Take care of the house, and above all—don't let anything happen to the girls. (leaves)

Pierrot

Oh, hang it! Leave it to me. If the girls deceive me, they'll have to be pretty smart. Still, it's a cursed cow to control, and by nature eels wriggle a lot. I'd better call Glandine and preach her a sermon.

(Glandine enters. Pierrot takes an armchair.)

Pierrot

Listen to me, Glandine. Honor is a joy, but a joy which spoils when exposed to the air. A girl is like a bottle of water of the Queen of Hungary—it loses its virtue if it is not shut tight. This is what caused a great philosopher to say that a woman must live shut in her room. He didn't speak of girls, for they were thinly sown in his days, more so than today.

Glendine

What are you trying to say with all your nonsense? Are you mad?

Pierrot

How—as if I were crazy! Don't you know that I am presently your pedagogue?

Glendine

I'm really in good hands.

Pierrot

I am of your opinion. What the bridle is to a horse, a stick to a blind man, a rudder to a ship: I am the bridle, you are the horse. I am the stick, you are the blind man. I am the rudder, you are the ship, but a rudder with which I will prevent you from going on the roads of men.— For the world is a sea and winds blow in this water which bubbles. I who have reason in this sea—I'm getting confused.

Glendine

Quickly, quickly, help—here's a man drowning.

Pierrot

Who's right, I say? Now, Harlequin left me in this house to protect you.

Glendine

I am much obliged to you, I assure you I will protect myself quite well.

Pierrot

Bah. If you please, I don't trust girls, I've been tricked before.

Glendine

What, you mean you have commerce with women?

Pierrot

Right, when one is made in a certain manner, one has to resell this merchandise. A little baggage begged me to give her a kiss—dammit, she didn't have to ask twice. I was neither mad or a fool. I approached, she gave me a big slap in the face. Since then, I've sworn never to kiss again.

Glendine

Good idea, Pierrot. Believe me, don't play with girls—there's nothing to be gained.

Pierrot

Yes, if it's only a slap. However, no more discussion: go in and march ahead of me. (he watches her go) Out of sight, as if swallowed.

CURTAIN

SCENE VI

Scene of bravery. Harlequin, dressed bravely as a soldier, is accompanied by Pasquariel and three other soldiers.

Harlequin

Hey, Hope, Chain Breaker, Gun Powder, Terror of Chickens? Well, my children, what does your heart say to you? Has it been a long while since you have eaten human flesh?

Pasquariel

You don't need to speak, my captain. I am beforehand with you. (draws his sword and makes a lazzi)

Harlequin

By God, here's a fine fellow, this comedian has killed more chickens by himself than my whole platoon together.

(Pasquariel makes yet more lazzi.)

Harlequin

Hola, hola, who is that man there? Don't let your ardor cool. Let's find Cinthio. Who is that man there? He seems to me to have the air of a seducer of girls. Who are you, my friend? Isn't your name Cinthio?

Cinthio (looking Harlequin up and down)

Hey, what's that to you?

Harlequin

Huh! Dammit—what's it to me? If you are Cinthio, or even only cousin, half cousin, or cousin germane to Cinthio, by God, may the devil take me, you will find out.

Cinthio

May one imagine, sir, as to how this Cinthio has offended you? For you seem to me quite enraged.

Harlequin

Assuredly I am enraged. Cinthio is a clown who goes from girl to girl with a revolving promise of marriage. Oh, God, if I meet you, my little friend, you will keep the word you gave to my sister, or you will get a whipping from me.

Cinthio

He is quite a rogue, to deceive girls like that.

Harlequin

I want him dead or alive. I would give a hundred crowns reward.

Cinthio

Hold on, sir. I want you to earn more than fifty louis today. Give me thirty and I will tell you where Cinthio is—and so, not to hold you forever in suspense—it's me.

Harlequin (astonished)

It's you, it's you! Ha, on my oath, I am delighted. You don't wish to marry my sister?

Cinthio

Really, as we are in a century where women—

Harlequin

No, oh, by God, we'll see. You will take her—when I make you swallow some medicine. Let me alone with him.

Cinthio

I laugh at your threats, and to show you I'm not afraid of you or your bullies—I will wait for you in that hotel.

Harlequin (to soldiers)

Let someone follow that man and prevent me from seeing him. There, by God, it's necessary to stir vigorously in an affair.

CURTAIN

SCENE VII

Scene of the Dutch. Mezzetin as a Dutch captain with a wooden leg.

Mezzetin

Guten tag, mein herr, guten tag.

Harlequin

Guten tag, guten tag.

Mezzetin

Mich, being a stranger seek lodging in this town.

Harlequin

This town, sir, is very obliged to you. There, my word, a cursed body—

Mezzetin

Show me, if you please, sir, where be lodging for my horse and me?

Harlequin

It's a hotel you seek, sir, right?

Mezzetin

Yes sir, a hotel.

Harlequin

Wait, sir, where you are, you will be fine. There's good cuisine here, and also you will find some pretty girls, and all that you want, I understand, immediately.

Mezzetin

I ask monsieur's excuse, coz I no speak good Frenchie—but my thinking is much better than my talking.

Harlequin

Go, sir, don't trouble yourself, believe me, sir, go stay in that hotel, for a man who has only one leg ought to be more tired than other people.

Mezzetin

Adieu, monsieur, I thank you, very strongly. (knocks at the door)

Harlequin

I really need to know who this stranger is who is going to put up in my hotel. Come here, sir. May one know where you're from and what brings you here?

Mezzetin

I am a Dutch gentleman from Dutchland, who comes to this city on a matter of great importance.

Harlequin

You see, it's one of those sots who are very self-important.

Mezzetin

I have been on sea duty and commanded a ship during a naval combat.

Harlequin

What the devil, sir, why are you here? Apparently you have a safe conduct?

Mezzetin

I have come expressly from my country to claim my vessel which these French devils have burned like a chicken.

Harlequin

Eh, you're right. They're nasty devils, these Frenchies. You should have cried fire—someone would have come to your aid.

Mezzetin

Not at all, sir. I have already lost my leg which those madmen have taken from me during the battle.

Harlequin

If you lost your leg, it's not my fault, I assure you, sir. I have not found it.

Mezzetin

I am going to claim my member at the court.

Harlequin

My word, sir, if I may speak openly, I don't believe they'll give it back.

Mezzetin

Hey, why, sir?

Harlequin

Well, sir, if the court had to return, to all brothers in

Holland, all the members that the Frenchies carried off this last year, hey, there wouldn't be any more legs in France.

Mezzetin

But, sir, how can I do my duty without limbs on a ship?

Harlequin

I advise you, sir, to serve in a hospital. From what I see, Mr. Dutchman, you've been a little dismantled. Ha, ha, ha.

Mezzetin

I don't laugh, sir, I am a gentleman, donner vette.

Harlequin

Donner vette, my little friend. You feel your old beating. I will send you back to Amsterdam.

(They fight. The Dutchman falls and makes many lazzi with his limb.)

CURTAIN

SCENE VIII

Scene of the Commissariat. Cinthio, Isabelle, Harlequin as the Commissariat, and Pierrot as clerk.

Harlequin

Come on, hurry up, draw your writing desk, close the door, put the dogs outside, wipe your nose, leave a wide margin, and write large and clear.

Pierrot (pulling a large desk and a tiny pen from within)

Sir, work quickly, if you please, I have short breath, as you know, which doesn't permit me to stay in one place very long.

Harlequin

I will be done soon. (to Cinthio) What's your name? Tell me your name, first name, occupation, country, street apartment number and parish. Do you have a father, mother, brothers or relatives? What brings you to Paris?

Have you been here long? Who do you visit? Where do you go? Where have you been? Write it down, quick. (he hits Pierrot on the shoulder)

Pierrot (falling down on his desk)

Ah, my shoulder's broken. Here's a crippled clerk.

Harlequin

That's the interrogatory method. What a stupid ignoramus. (to Cinthio) And you, my little squire, you don't wish to respond? Write that he said nothing.

Cinthio

What do you want, sir?

Harlequin

Silence! You suppose, my friend, that I have the time to listen to all your stupidities? Do you know that I have three rogues to hang today already, not counting you?

Pierrot

And five or six ladies to dispossess, or drive crazy.

Cinthio

Sir, my name's Cinthio and I lodge with Harlequin.

Pierrot

I know him. He's a rogue.

Harlequin (giving him another blow)

Think what you're doing, you beast! Would you know this so-called lady here? (pointing to Isabelle) And you, pretty one, with becoming eyes, would you know this pilgrim hoodlum?

Isabelle

Alas sir. I know him only too well. He's the ingrate who deceived me with a promise of marriage.

Pierrot

This affair looks very dark.

Harlequin

If all the girls of today had as many husbands as they do promises of marriage, they'd have near enough to change like the weather. (towards a clerk) Go tell the chain gang not to leave yet. I have another one for them. (to Isabelle) But, is your story real?

Isabelle

Wait, sir. Here, read.

Harlequin (opening a paper)

I am very embarrassed. For two days, I've had a rheumatic which prevents me from seeing well.

(The clerk who went out returns.)

Clerk

Sir, the chain gang won't go until you do.

Harlequin (to Pierrot)

Wait, read this.

Pierrot

Me, sir? You know quite well I have never learned to read.

Harlequin (to Isabelle)

Read it then. I cede my judicial rights to you.

Pierrot (writing)

The one who admits not to know how to read or write, owing to his judicial rank.

Isabelle

I subscribe.

Harlequin (to Cinthio)

And that's all that's required. What do you say to that, Mr. Rogue?

Cinthio

I say, sir, that no one treats a person of my quality in this manner.

Harlequin

Ah, my little companion, you wish to make a joke; let's go see if you look funny dancing from the end of a rope.

Isabelle

No, Mr. Commissar, there is no punishment cruel enough to punish his perfidy. To what has my despair reduced me? I left my family to follow him. I've been exposed to a thousand hazards, for you know the risks that a girl runs by herself.

Harlequin

She runs even more when she is with someone.

Isabelle

I became a wench in the inn of Harlequin, where I hid my name under that of Glandine. He came to lodge in this hotel, for his misfortune and for mine. For it is very hard to see someone hang—someone one so tenderly loves—boo hoo. (she cries)

Pierrot (crying)

Boo, hoo.

Harlequin (toward Cinthio)

You will pay for making my secretary cry, rogue. Make the rope extra thick. Here's a rogue who's got a tough neck to break.

Cinthio

I admit my fault, but, Mr. Commissar, you have to pardon love.

(Cinthio draws a purse and gives money to the Commissar.)

Harlequin (taking the money)

No, no, I claim to do my duty honorably. I will use this money to give you a fancy funeral.

Cinthio

But, Mr. Commissar, give me quarter. I am ready to marry her.

Pierrot

He's right. It's better to marry than hang.

Isabelle

Me, traitor, marry you after all your infidelities? I renounce your love, I don't want a heart as corrupt as yours.

Cinthio (on his knees)

Ah, mercy, miss, may love make you forget a crime that love itself has committed.

(Harlequin and Pierrot are also throwing themselves on their knees.)

Harlequin

Listen, miss, if he hangs you won't be any fatter. You've done enough.

Pierrot

Provided he pays handsomely for my writings, I advise you to forgive him. It's punishment enough to have a wife.

Isabelle

Ingrate, I ought to hate you, but I feel I don't.

Harlequin

Ah, then you're good friends. Presently the business may be wound up. It is right to tell you that the Commissar and the clerk are impostors, who put on these clothes to make you marry.

Cinthio

It's true, my word. A procedure that's cost me quite a bit of trouble.

Harlequin

Sir, in honor of this wedding, we must entertain ourselves. Come, bring on the band and call in everybody in the inn.

(All the comedians leave with guitars and parody big bands.)

Chorus

Follow, follow, love,

Let us become inflamed.

Oh, oh, oh, how sweet

It is to love.

Mezzetin (singing)

For Hymen one is destined.

All the same,

Sing a song.

Goddam, let Glandine love,

For in her season,

She'll play mischief

And have a son like herself.

Chorus

Follow, follow, love,

Let us become inflamed.

Oh, oh, oh, how sweet

It is to love.

Hymen

A girl is vain to pretend

Marriage is charming.

Vain for her to contradict.

He wishes her a lover

And nothing is so much to be feared

As the age of fifteen years.

Chorus

Follow, follow, love,

Let us become inflamed.

Oh, oh, oh, how sweet

It is to love.

Trio

A lover in the woods,

Sick of chasing,

Wants to give up the prize.

But one isn't made of wood,

And sometimes one makes a mistake.

Chorus

Follow, follow, love,

Let us become inflamed.

Oh, oh, oh, how sweet

It is to love.

CURTAIN

THE ABDUCTIONS
BY MICHEL BARON

CAST OF CHARACTERS

de la Davoisier

de la Sozière

The Count, son of Davoisier

The Chevalier, son of Davoisier

Leonor, daughter of de la Sozière

Guillaume, Farmer of Mr. de la Davoisier

Babit, Guillaume's daughter

Pellerin, old servant of Mr. de la Davoisier

Vincent, peasant

Pierrot, peasant

THE PLAY

The action takes place in the Château of de la Davoisier.

GUILLAUME

I admit, sir, that the year has not been bad, and that I've earned something with you. Hey, what would it be, in the end, if I was always ruined?

DAVOISIER

Come, come, Mr. Guillaume, let's speak honestly: you've never lost anything with me, and I'm not angry for that, I swear to you. I'm not even saying that to oblige you in the future to hold my land at higher rent.

GUILLAUME

Another, perhaps, would give you more for them and not pay you so well.

DAVOISIER

That's what I consider. There's no need for caution with you, and one can say here that the farmer is richer than the master. Your daughter Babit, if you continue, will have the biggest share of the province.

GUILLAUME

Hey, mercy, sir, spare me.

DAVOISIER

I'm not joking.

GUILLAUME

Hey, sir, I'm not as rich as they imagine, and if I were, who would cast their eyes on a poor peasant girl?

DAVOISIER

Listen—before one would have been capable of making some scruple, yes, and I have seen in my times that it would be a great crime to marry beneath one—but now, all that is completely changed.

GUILLAUME

Oh, well, sir, as for me, it is permitted to think this over—if it was once a crime for a man of condition to marry a rich peasant, then it was a great stupidity for a peasant to give his daughter to a gentleman; and indeed, I have not forgotten from where I came, and that one lives happily only with his equals.

DAVOISIER

Goodbye, Mr. Guillaume—take good care of my affairs, Pellerin, I am going to dine with Mr. de la Marcelière—I may indeed sup there, Have you had Superb saddled?

PELLERIN

Yes, sir, but I'm afraid one ought to be constrained to change that name a little. The poor animal's beginning to feel his age—and his repeated genuflections will make you confess, perhaps at your expense; names like Humble or Civil would better suit him.

DAVOISIER

I has not yet noticed that.

PELLERIN

So much the better for you.

DAVOISIER

Mr. Guillaume, arrange all your receipts and I will sign them on my return.

GUILLAUME

Yes, sir.

DAVOISIER

Pellerin, you will tell my wife where I went.

PELLERIN

Yes, sir.

DAVOISIER

Mr. Guillaume, send Babit to the Château to divert her; a poor patient is ravished to have someone to amuse her.

GUILLAUME

I won't fail.

DAVOISIER

Pellerin, the daughter of Mr. de la Sozière, my intended daughter-in-law ought to come to see my wife; tell my son, the Count, not to go out today so he'll be here to receive her.

PELLERIN

Suffice, sir.

DAVOISIER

Mr. Guillaume, I still have something to tell you.

GUILLAUME

Whatever you please.

DAVOISIER

I will remember, Pellerin?

PELLERIN

Sir?

DAVOISIER

Be careful that my son, the Chevalier, doesn't do anything stupid.

PELLERIN

I'll keep an eye on him.

DAVOISIER

Ah, I remember, Mr. Guillaume—don't forget to go— one of these days this week—to go by the Moulin Rouge and see if there's something that needs to be done.

GUILLAUME

I will. Go, sir.

DAVOISIER

Wait—is that all? Yes—goodbye.

(Exit Davoisier)

PELLERIN

Mr. Guillaume, would you allow Pellerin to congratulate you on grand alliances into which good fortune may make you enter. Our master is indeed right: your daughter Babit is not going to be badly chased by all our starveling gentlemen hereabouts.

GUILLAUME

My poor Pellerin, you take me for a great fool if you think I'm bull-headed about these chimeras.

PELLERIN

Oh—sir—I take you for what you are—that is to say, a man marvelously astute in all affairs.

GUILLAUME

I'd be making a fine show of it, my word.

PELLERIN

Listen, after some consideration—

GUILLAUME

I would be making a slave of myself.

PELLERIN

I wouldn't disapprove right away.

GUILLAUME

So others can enjoy the fruits of my labors.

PELLERIN

Frankly, that's not easy to see—

GUILLAUME

My daughter's children will be much greater lords than me?

PELLERIN

There are lots of things to say on that topic.

GUILLAUME

I will call them "sir"?

PELLERIN

It's true.

GUILLAUME

I'd have to get out of the way if they have company?

PELLERIN

It's certain—

GUILLAUME

I wouldn't say the least word, because it would cause laughter.

PELLERIN

I see.

GUILLAUME

Not the least little familiarity.

PELLERIN

I wouldn't worry about that.

GUILLAUME

I wouldn't drink with my son-in-law.

PELLERIN

What appearance—

GUILLAUME

Not the least little game of horseshoes?

PELLERIN

Truly—

GUILLAUME

With ladies.

PELLERIN

Why—

GUILLAUME

At cards?

PELLERIN

Yes.

GUILLAUME

A stroll?

PELLERIN

What?

GUILLAUME

No, Pellerin—you will see this is useless. I'll never do it while I have my head.

PELLERIN

Hey! Who the devil told you otherwise?

GUILLAUME

You—who for the last hour only argued with me.

PELLERIN

I've been telling you you are right for the last hour,

GUILLAUME

I read some portion of a beautiful sentence. Ah, it was completely beautiful.

PELLERIN

Oh, I believe it.

GUILLAUME

Oh, completely beautiful.

PELLERIN

Say it, will you?

GUILLAUME

Here it is: "Whoever enters the house of a great man becomes a serf." It's Plutarch who said that beautiful thing.

PELLERIN

And Plutarch wasn't wrong.

GUILLAUME

It's around twenty years ago that one of the friends of a great lord that I was serving no longer wanted to go to the château of my master when they were supposed to spend a few days together. Passing through Angers, they unfortunately found in a cabaret an open Plutarch, and friend of my master, who wasn't such a great lord as he; casting his eyes by chance on this sentence, he no longer wished to pursue the trip, although he was only four short leagues from his house.

PELLERIN

This friend was a man of good sense, and frankly, sir, I sense much better than you, what sort of sauce they lard on servitude—it's always frightful, and in the end, people of wit must serve only so as not to serve any more.

GUILLAUME

That's what I've done, and I hope before too long to no longer need to meddle in business, and become absolutely my own master.

PELLERIN

That's wisely considered, and if I were you, I would take for my son-in-law someone who would be capable of serving me in my old age.

GUILLAUME

Indeed, that's what I'm plotting.

PELLERIN

Someone who'd be nice to me—

GUILLAUME

That's what I intend.

PELLERIN

With concern and even submission.

GUILLAUME

Assuredly.

PELLERIN

Who loved me.

GUILLAUME

Yes.

PELLERIN

Who would make me the godfather of his first child.

GUILLAUME

That's just what I intend.

PELLERIN

You see that I know what you need.

GUILLAUME

That's true.

PELLERIN

In the end a man who gets all his fortune from me.

GUILLAUME

Hem!

PELLERIN

What?

GUILLAUME

What are you saying?

PELLERIN

I am saying that you won't take as much care—

GUILLAUME

Oh—pardon me, pardon me.

PELLERIN

I don't yet have any—

GUILLAUME

So it's not you that I'm looking as for my son-in-law.

PELLERIN

Yet, come to think of it, I have all the characteristics—

GUILLAUME

That doesn't suffice—

PELLERIN

Hey, why's that?

GUILLAUME

Hey—I don't know, Pellerin.

(Exit Guillaume)

PELLERIN (alone)

So there go all my efforts broken, and charming Babit will be for someone other than myself. I'm furious! Never mind, so long as it won't be Pierrot or Vincent who marries her, I am half-consoled. Known rivals, and of our situation—almost—that seems to me to be more painful than others. I will be so well in that way, that at least I won't be ashamed to cede her to the one who gets her. Still, one can judge as to where her inclinations incline—and the poor little thing doesn't yet know that she has a heart—or at least she's unaware as to what use one puts it. That poor child, how pretty she is. Why suppose I abducted her. Right! But that old geezer is as obstinate as the devil, and I'd be afraid that he'd have me abducted in my turn, for trying to raise myself a bit higher than I ought. I must be devilishly amorous, for quite dangerous enterprises are passing through my mind.

(Enter the Count)

COUNT

Pellerin, Pellerin!

PELLERIN

Sir—

COUNT

Go quickly into the courtyard of the Château.

PELLERIN

What am I to do there?

COUNT

Go quickly.

(as Pellerin starts to leave)

Where are you off to?

PELLERIN

I'm rushing where you told me.

COUNT

First, learn what I want you to do.

PELLERIN

I thought I only had to rush.

COUNT

You will find Leonor who's going to come out of the carriage—lead her to my mother's room, and tell her—be sure of this—that I went out hunting—because I don't wish to see her.

PELLERIN

Hey, why, if you please?—aren't you quite ready to marry her?

COUNT

Don't waste time—do what I tell you, and come find me: I will indeed inform you of things.

PELLERIN

I'll be back right away.

COUNT (alone)

Ah, if I were as close to marrying Leonor as my father imagines, my wishes, my tenderness, my efforts are leading me far astray. I don't wish to do myself an eternal misfortune; I no longer love her, or rather I never loved her—since I never felt what I feel today.

How many reactions I was unaware of! How much unease, how many alarms, how many sighs!— No, Leonor, I never loved you—

PELLERIN (returning)

Sir, I acquitted myself of the errand you gave me. If you had seen her, sir, what sadness spread over the face of Madame Leonor! If you had witnessed her sighs when I told her—

COUNT

Shut up! I don't want to listen to you anymore. What you are saying will give me pain—and won't change the decision I've made.

PELLERIN

What decision, I beg you?

COUNT

I no longer intend to marry her. I'm in love elsewhere.

PELLERIN

And with whom, by all the devils?

COUNT

With Babit.

PELLERIN

With Babit.

COUNT

With herself.

PELLERIN

That's all I need.

COUNT

My dear Pellerin—what must I do?—because, in the end, I adore her.

PELLERIN

My word, sir, I see nothing here that's very troubling.

COUNT

My dear child, I have recourse only in you.

PELLERIN

But before getting involved in it, it would be nice, it seems to me, to know what you want—what you intend to do with Babit—because, in the end, I don't want to do anything that wounds my conscience.

COUNT

What do I want to do, Pellerin? Love her, serve her, adore her, respect her as all that I have most dear in the world.

PELLERIN

Now those are the most beautiful words in the world, but if I am not mistaken, I didn't hear you proffer the essentials.

COUNT

Huh? What do you want me to say?

PELLERIN

Hey, guess.

COUNT

Don't make me languish. What more must be done?

PELLERIN

What more must be done?

COUNT

Yes.

PELLERIN

Marry her.

COUNT

That's just what I intend.

PELLERIN

Oh, in that case don't put yourself in pain; all you have to do is to let me do it. Yes. No. He will never do it. He will never consent to it, I tell you—he wouldn't do it to an enemy of Mr. de la Sozière. On the other hand, you run no risk that is certain, Are you very much in love?

COUNT

One cannot be more than I am.

PELLERIN

You must abduct Babit—it's the quickest way. I advise you as if for myself.

COUNT

I was thinking of that already.

PELLERIN

You see how fine minds meet. Oh—in that case, since you are so well resolved on the thing, you have only to find yourself the six and a half hours needed to do it. Plague, it already needs a day—or seven hours.— That won't be bad; you have, I tell you—only to be near the big walnut tree that you see here in this Isle—at the hour that I set, I will find some way to make her prowl around there—or actually stroll with her. I will lead her there myself. Hide yourself carefully behind the hedge, and your horse, too. When you have seized her, you will arrange things after that as you wish.

COUNT

I can rely on you?

PELLERIN

It's worth doing.

COUNT

You will remember?

PELLERIN

Hey, yes, I tell you—get moving. I see your little brother the Chevalier coming here. He'll soon suspect, maybe, that I am the one who gave you this fine advice; but God watch over me, I am not capable of that.

COUNT

Goodbye, then.

(The Count leaves)

PELLERIN

On my word, poor Guillaume, as well as I, counted without his host; he didn't want gentlemen—he'll soon have one. I wanted to marry his daughter; I'm quite far from it. I don't know how to take a step that doesn't fall back on me.

CHEVALIER (entering)

Where is she? Hey, my God—won't I meet her again?

PELLERIN

Who?

CHEVALIER

The one I'm looking for.

PELLERIN

Who are you searching for?

CHEVALIER

I'm searching—

PELLERIN

I'm searching, I'm searching—for two or three years you were searching for a whipping, but now that you've begun to get big, that you have the key to your parts, you make fun of everyone. Why don't you go study your fortifications? Why don't you finish this which has been laid out on the table for so long? At least, Mr. Chevalier, you know that it is your father who authorized me to speak to you as I do. What are you amusing yourself with? He will not scold baby when he sees nothing's been done.

CHEVALIER

My poor Pellerin, I cast myself at your knees.

PELLERIN

Go on, get up—I won't tell him anything of your pranks.

CHEVALIER

That's not what's causing me despair.

PELLERIN

Perhaps you want to go see one of your comrades? Go, go—I won't tell him.

CHEVALIER

My poor Pellerin, that's not it.

PELLERIN

Do you need some money? I don't have any, but all the same—

CHEVALIER

You are not penetrating the depth of my heart.

PELLERIN

Oh, yeah? Have you met with some annoyance?

CHEVALIER

I am in despair.

PELLERIN

Madame your mother has quarreled with you?

CHEVALIER

You haven't said anything of what's causing my sorrow.

PELLERIN

Oh, in that case say it yourself, because, on my word, I'm at my wit's end.

CHEVALIER

Ah, Pellerin.

PELLERIN

What's wrong?

CHEVALIER

I see—

PELLERIN

Well?

CHEVALIER

I see—

PELLERIN

What do you see?

CHEVALIER

I tell you I see—

PELLERIN

Ah, by my word—I see, I see—I see that I don't see very much, either.

CHEVALIER

My poor Pellerin, don't abandon me.

PELLERIN

What then is to be said?

CHEVALIER

Babit—Pellerin, one more time—Babit.

BABIT (entering)

Sir—

CHEVALIER

Don't go away, Pellerin.

PELLERIN

Well, Pellerin, Pellerin—what is it?

CHEVALIER

I am lost.

PELLERIN

These poor kids. They don't know how to take it. By my word, they make me pity them. Both of 'em—look a bit—end all this.

(Babit enters)

BABIT

What is it you want with me, Chevalier?

CHEVALIER

I would really like for you to stay seated—there—for a while.

BABIT

I don't know. I'm going to find Madame to divert her a little.

CHEVALIER

Stay here for a moment, I beg you.

BABIT

Mr. Chevalier, don't come near me.

CHEVALIER

Allow me to speak to you.

BABIT

I'll call my father! Father!

CHEVALIER

Well, no—I won't come near you. But let me look at you.

BABIT

Be quick about it.

CHEVALIER

Ah, Babit, how you hate me.

BABIT

Me? Not at all, I don't hate you.

CHEVALIER

Let me kiss your hand.

BABIT

Father!

CHEVALIER

Well, no, no, no. Babit—would you like me to give you candies?

BABIT

No.

CHEVALIER

I've got some little green apricots here; would you like them?

BABIT

No.

CHEVALIER

Would you like an orange?

BABIT

No.

CHEVALIER

In that case, what would you like me to give you?

BABIT

Nothing.

CHEVALIER

Babit, the brocade of your waist is not pretty, and I have the wherewithal—if you like, you can make a much nicer one.

BABIT

My father won't allow me to take anything.

CHEVALIER

He won't know it comes from me, Babit. I will make my mother give it to you. Would you like it? Speak!

BABIT

Yes.

CHEVALIER

Will you love me, after that, Babit?

BABIT

Yes.

CHEVALIER

With all your heart?

BABIT

Yes.

CHEVALIER

Will you come stroll in the Isle with me?

BABIT

No.

CHEVALIER

Ah, Babit, do you want me to despair?

BABIT

No.

CHEVALIER

I assure you, anyway, that if you won't allow me to kiss your hand, I'm going to die.

BABIT

I don't want you to die.

CHEVALIER

Ah, my dear Babit.

BABIT

I never wanted to let the Count kiss it, and yes, he said as much to me.

PELLERIN

Courage—this is not going badly, you have only to continue. Plague, my little gentleman, what a tender manner you have.

CHEVALIER

What tone are you taking?

PELLERIN

I am within my rights to reprimand you. Your father, you know, gave me that duty, and these are not the example that this philosopher held up to you, and we gave you. And you, sweet pretty, who thus gave your hand to kiss—who showed you how to do it?

CHEVALIER

Oh, I beg you, quarrel with me as much as you like, but let your wrath respect her.

PELLERIN

I intend to speak to her. All these intrigues—

CHEVALIER

I won't suffer it, I tell you, and despite my father's orders, I'll make you repent of it, if you say a single word to her.

BABIT

Sir, sir? Pellerin, don't squabble; I'm going to find Madame.

(Babit leaves)

CHEVALIER

You triumph at last, there she goes, but you won't get any further by it. I mean to tell you so, and despite your efforts, your vigilance, and the threats of my father, I shall love her, I shall serve her, I shall adore her the rest of my life.

PELLERIN

What's going on? What's that mean? Is this the way one ought to speak?

CHEVALIER

Well, I was wrong, I confess it, I'll change the topic: and I beg you in the name of whatever can touch you further—first of all, don't tell my father about this, and I entreat you, you who took so much trouble over me in my youth, don't ruin in a moment the entire fruit of your efforts—and serve me in my love.

PELLERIN

He's making me enter into his sorrows. Well, who would ever have thought of this little traitor? It's only two years since I was whipping him. What speech, what transports! I am completely stupefied, and I feel he's debauching me, too.

CHEVALIER

Heavens, look you, if you don't serve me, my poor Pellerin, I will kill myself.

PELLERIN

I can no longer stand it; he's wrenching tears from me.

CHEVALIER

If you have in your heart some friendship for me—

PELLERIN

Get up.

CHEVALIER

Will you feel for my sighs?

PELLERIN

Yes.

CHEVALIER

I shall obtain from you the help that I implore?

PELLERIN

Yes.

CHEVALIER

In the end, you'll do things in a way so that I'll be happy?

PELLERIN

Oh—get up, I tell you.

CHEVALIER

Oh, my dear Pellerin, how obliged I'll be to you.

PELLERIN

Heavens. If he came out of me, I couldn't feel more tenderness. I held him in my arms for such a long time.

CHEVALIER

Remember, carefully, what you have promised me.

PELLERIN

Yes, I will remember. But, there's no time to waste; your brother is in love with Babit, and just like you, I promised to serve him. What to do? He must be informed. I half see someone. At seven o'clock at least, you will bring her here.

CHEVALIER

Won't you come with me?

PELLERIN

No, I will stay here to straighten out all these affairs. Go, I tell you, withdraw.

I wasn't mistaken, and it's precisely the intended spouse of the Count.

(Leonor enters)

LEONOR

Mr. Chevalier, haven't you seen the Count?

CHEVALIER

Madame, it seems to me I saw him just now strolling towards the woods.

PELLERIN

You are mistaken, for he left this morning for the hunt.

CHEVALIER

I'm not at all mistaken, it was he.

PELLERIN

Nonetheless, he told me that he was going hunting.

LEONOR

He told you to say that he had gone there.

PELLERIN

It must have been something like that.

LEONOR

Oh, assuredly. Pellerin, listen. Chevalier—would you like for me actually to say something to him?

CHEVALIER

Willingly, Madame; I am withdrawing. Pellerin, at least I will do all you told me.

PELLERIN

I really like that—do it, I will take care of the rest.

CHEVALIER

Madame, I give you good-day.

LEONOR

I am going to rejoin you soon. Oh, indeed, Pellerin, good faith is necessary here; indeed, I see things here that you are unaware of, and it's perhaps you who are managing the intrigue. I have, instead of believing it, seen at least though the mystery you've come yourself to make me. The Count, you said, had gone to the hunt, and I saw him strolling from the window where I was; here already, a lie. A person who is suspicious, is not long in discovering things that she needs to know.

PELLERIN

I am giving myself to the Devil. Madame, if I understand anything at all of what you are doing—

LEONOR

Here is what will make you understand—hold on.

(gives him money)

PELLERIN

Effectively, this marvelously opens the mind.

LEONOR

Do you want to serve me?

PELLERIN

With all my heart.

LEONOR

But sincerely.

PELLERIN

You have only to speak. Are you in love with Babit?

LEONOR

This is not a question of Babit.

PELLERIN

It's Babit who is the malady of this country here.

LEONOR

Meaning that the Count is in love with her!

PELLERIN

You said it.

LEONOR

Indeed, you see that I have been a long while without noticing this change. You know, as well as I do, that my reputation is very interested in all this because to suffer that an affair which has dragged on for so long to break without apparent cause— If I had for the Count anything except indifference and even scorn— for he doesn't deserve for me to have other feelings for him—when I ought to have hate— I must have some urgings that— And the dazzle that our marriage has caused in the whole province no longer allows me to take another decision henceforth.

PELLERIN

Meaning that you want to marry him at whatever the price may be.

LEONOR

Or throw myself in a convent for the rest of my life.

PELLERIN

Oh, by my honor, keep yourself from it—that would be a shame.

LEONOR

In that case, figure out what we can do before this coldness which the Count has for me increases.

PELLERIN

And if I did things so that your marriage was concluded as of this evening—what would you give me?

LEONOR

I would give you more than you dare to hope for.

PELLERIN

Listen, without wasting time you must— Hey, the Devil—it's impossible to be alone for a moment. Madame, with your permission, Pierrot dwells here—I am going to rejoin you

(aside)

And I will show you what to do to get a nasty beating.

(aloud)

Here, you see this peasant—he's one of the rivals of the Count.

LEONOR

Just God!

PELLERIN

Let's step to the side for fear this scoundrel hears us.

(Exit Leonor)

PIERROT

By God, we'll see what Mr. Pellerin has done; he promised me that he would tell Babit that I love her a lot; we will see what his eloquence has produced. Perhaps I would have done better to speak to her myself. It's always better not to employ anyone except oneself in these affairs, and I fear having entrusted myself to the fox. But all means are valuable, there's nothing lost. What I haven't done, I will do.

PELLERIN

At least don't fail to inform your father.— Well, what is this, Pierrot? What will you give me for such good news?

PIERROT

Hot damn! You must tell me what it is first.

PELLERIN

No, I want to know before what you will give me.

PIERROT

Oh—doggone, don't be such a clown. Tell me right away.

PELLERIN

Then beg me very hard.

PIERROT

Oh—doggone—lookie here. I don't know such ceremonies—tell me what you want.

PELLERIN

In that case, you shan't know.

PIERROT

Jimminy, I don't know how to make manners, and I'm going without so much as a preamble to ask her of her father.

PELLERIN

You'll spoil everything.

PIERROT

Never mind—I know how to get what I want.

PELLERIN

Come, come, Pierrot, I took pity on you.

PIERROT

Oh, well—say then first what you just told me.

PELLERIN

You are going to put your business in a situation that can no longer be fixed; I have sounded Babit's father on your subject. First of all, he made me see many difficulties—but in the end I did so well that I made him speak, and after several epithets, of a blunt booby, of a high horse, of a fat peasant, and some others, about which I did honor to your modesty, he declared to me quite bluntly that he'd sooner strangle his daughter than give her to you.

PIERROT

Is this the fine news you had to give me?— Hot damn!— Let it go whistle: one is always doing honor to someone to seek their daughters, If he's so rich, let him eat twice. Come what garden, there are cabbages; if I don't have this one, will have another one. Goodbye, Pellerin, until I see you again, I won't always be so unhappy, doggone—I'm being made fun of!

PELLERIN

Oh! Oh! Pierrot, you are really hasty: you are leaving.

PIERROT

Yes, by Heck!

PELLERIN

You insist on knowing the rest!

PIERROT

And there's still something more?

PELLERIN

You are not so unlucky as you believe.

PIERROT

Eh, why?

PELLERIN

I kept the good part for last.

PIERROT

Speak up quick.

PELLERIN

Babit, despite the decision of her father, doesn't want to have anyone but you.

PIERROT

For real?

PELLERIN

It's so true, that at seven o'clock, if you stay under the great elm down there, Babit will be there to declare to you her feelings.

PIERROT

Yes, hot damn! I'll be there!

PELLERIN

But listen, a bit—the way you are dressed—look—

PIERROT

I'll put on my Sunday clothes.

PELLERIN

That's not what she wants. Whatever's done tonight at seven o'clock—never mind—she fears being surprised with you—she wants you to be disguised as a girl—at least that way, if someone surprises you, they won't suspect her of being with a man.

PIERROT

Gosh—she's not wrong. I'm going to think a bit about all this.

PELLERIN

At seven o'clock?

PIERROT

Go, go—don't put yourself in any pain over it.

(Exit Pierrot)

PELLERIN

By Jove, today I'm going to make the happiness or misfortune of many folks—but it still remains to punish one of my rivals; he will feel a bit of all this. Where will I find him now? I wager he's seeking me. Oh, by Jove, Mr. Vincent, it won't help you any, being the notary of our town; you will learn what it is to dare to attack me. I think that I will do better to go find him myself. But here he is—apropos.

(Enter Vincent)

Oh, indeed, Vincent, my friend, it's almost seven, hurry up—it's almost night—be under that elm—Babit will be there right away.

VINCENT

Ah, Mr. Pellerin, how obliged I am to you.

PELLERIN

Go, I tell you, don't waste time—she wants to speak to you, she will show you what I cannot speak to you about.

VINCENT

Holy cow, Mr. Pellerin, yes, I'm gonna marry her—go—we won't drink badly together.

PELLERIN

Go, go, then.

VINCENT

All I got do is go there now?

PELLERIN

Wait until it gets a bit darker.

VINCENT

Then I'll actually have time to go fix a bench in my uncle's garden?

PELLERIN

Yes, yes, go. I will go now to inform Babit.

VINCENT

Goodbye, Mr. Pellerin.

PELLERIN

Goodbye, Vincent.

(Exit Vincent)

PELLERIN

Now, God be thanked, affairs are in the best condition in the world, and I think I see Mr. Guillaume at his door—I won't have the trouble of going to see him.— Hola, Mr. Guillaume, a word, mercy.— He has to be kept from home long enough to give the Chevalier time to convince Babit to come with him.

GUILLAUME

What do you want?

PELLERIN

To speak to you for a moment.

GUILLAUME

Well—I'm listening to you.

PELLERIN

Don't go home.

GUILLAUME

And the reason?

PELLERIN

When one is so close to one's home, domestic affairs occupy us—one is never attentive to what one is told, but is completely distracted. If a woman quarrels, one wants to hear what she says; if someone comes in or goes out, one seeks the cause; even the yelp of a dog gives unease. And as what I have to tell you demands complete attention, I would be quite easy that nothing disturb us.

Here we are now at a distance that's almost reasonable.

GUILLAUME

Here's a mountain that's going to give birth to a mouse.

PELLERIN

I don't do or say anything without a reason.

GUILLAUME

Let's see, will you.

PELLERIN

I begin. Despite the disobliging manner with which you received my proposals for your daughter Babit, I always let you have everything which concerns you with a devotion that is without parallel.

GUILLAUME

Where the Devil is this going?

PELLERIN

And about certain little flirtations between Vincent and Babit, about which I noticed several days ago.— I wanted to get to the bottom of things, and I've done so much that I've discovered a rendezvous between them today—at seven o'clock.

GUILLAUME

A rendezvous today at seven o'clock?

PELLERIN

Yes, sir—but I think it's no crime.

GUILLAUME

What do you mean it's no crime?

PELLERIN

No, sir—she's probably only there for a conversation.

GUILLAUME

Conversation with Vincent! Come, come, quick—let's not waste time, tell me the place at least— A stick, a stick. Speak—show me the place.

PELLERIN

Sir, I won't tell you until first you've promised me not to use that stick—except on Vincent.

GUILLAUME

Yes, yes— I promise you, whatever you like.

PELLERIN

For your daughter, a few slaps wouldn't do her ill.

GUILLAUME

Leave it to me. Where must I go?

PELLERIN

Under the big elm, down there. I cannot point it out to you—the night's too dark—but they must pass this way—we'll hear them come. Listen—I hear someone—stay put.

(aloud)

Is it you, Vincent?

VINCENT

Yes.

PELLERIN (as Vincent leaves)

Time to march—it's Vincent. All this, as you see, is in order—the gallant will be first at the rendezvous.

GUILLAUME

But my daughter's not coming?

PELLERIN

I hear someone—it's she, no question. Yes, go, follow her. Don't make any noise—on tiptoe, walk gently, strike hard, and don't fail to make the hunt pass by here.

GUILLAUME

I'll do it.

(Pierrot passes disguised as a woman. Guillaume walks stealthily behind him.)

PELLERIN (alone)

Come on, let's be prepared and not let them pass this way without being noticed. Good foot, good eye—ah, by Jove, I see them drubbing people. I believe the tragedy has already begun. I hear shouting, I hear running.

(Enter Vincent)

VINCENT

Yie! Yie! Yie!

PELLERIN

Ah, it's my trick here.

VINCENT

Ah, murder, they're smashing me.

PELLERIN

That scoundrel. How the devil does he scream like

that?

VINCENT

Ah, my arms are broken.

PELLERIN

Here he is.

VINCENT

Yie, yie, yie—so many blows, I'm dead.

PELLERIN

Ah, I'm furious not to have seen better what I did—he wouldn't have got off so lightly.

GUILLAUME (entering with Pierrot)

Ah, ah—little villain. So you give rendezvous?

PELLERIN

Here's Mr. Guillaume coming.

GUILLAUME

Ah, I'll teach you.

PIERROT

Father, I beg your pardon.

GUILLAUME

Ah, ah—slut!

PIERROT

Father, yie, yie, yie!

GUILLAUME

Ah, what do I see? Here's the work of Pellerin. But he will pay me—on my word.

VINCENT

Holy cow, what a fine opportunity missed! Damn—if I could only find Babit.

PIERROT

I hear Vincent; let's divert ourselves.

VINCENT

Who's there?

PIERROT

A friend.

VINCENT

Is it not my dear Babit?

PIERROT

Yes, Vincent.

VINCENT

Oh—hot damn! Will you come with me?

PIERROT

I wouldn't dare.

VINCENT

Oh—holy cow, will you come?

PIERROT

Ha, ha, ha!

PELLERIN

Oh, my word, this is completely funny. I do not know what the Chevalier will have done—but I gave him sufficient time.

DAVOISIER (entering)

Pellerin, what's all this?

PELLERIN

What?

SOZIÈRE

There was no need for your son to abduct my daughter, since I intended to give her to him.

DAVOISIER

I don't understand a thing.

GUILLAUME

Ah, ah, ah—I am ruined—unhappy father that I am. What will become of me?

DAVOISIER

What's the matter?

GUILLAUME

Ah, sir, my daughter has been abducted.

DAVOISIER

Your daughter's been abducted?

GUILLAUME

Yes, sir, and it's your son the Chevalier who abducted

her.

DAVOISIER

My son, the Chevalier?

PIERROT

Help! Help!

DAVOISIER

Now what is it?

PIERROT

Vincent is trying to abduct me.

SOZIÈRE

Why, what do I see—my daughter dressed as a peasant girl?

LEONOR (entering with the Count)

Yes, father, and if I hadn't used this method, I would have lost the Count forever.

DAVOISIER

What is this, Count?

COUNT

Father, I confess to you that I allowed myself to be taken with the charms of Babit. I had to abduct her. Pellerin was supposed to lead her to the place where I was waiting for her, and I don't know how it happened—I abducted Leonor in her place.

GUILLAUME

Ah, traitor, it's you who managed all this intrigue—but I'll have you hanged if you don't tell me where my daughter is.

DAVOISIER

Don't get carried away, Mr. Guillaume; I don't see anything terrible in all this. The Chevalier abducted your daughter—he'll have to marry her. You have money, make an effort, and all things will arrange themselves nicely.

GUILLAUME

Indeed, I have to agree to it, despite myself.

PELLERIN

Gentlemen, since you are all in agreement, thank me. I am the one who managed this business. I'm going to make the Chevalier and Babit come.

(Pellerin goes out)

SOZIÈRE

I'm delighted that all this is ending this way.

VINCENT

It looks to me as if only Pierrot and I are to be pitied.

PELLERIN (returning)

Come on, enter. Everything is arranged.

BABIT

Father, I ask you forgiveness.

GUILLAUME

Indeed, I have to forgive you.

CHEVALIER

Father—

DAVOISIER

Go, go—I am pleased.

PELLERIN

You are doing well because I fear the marriage may

need to be advanced a bit. See, it's my cleverness that makes several marriages in one day. Sir Count and Madame Leonor, Mr. Chevalier and Madame Babit—all that remains is for Vincent to marry Pierrot, and I will marry Guillaume.

PIERROT

G'wan, g'wan, keep it up. You're gonna pay me for this.

DAVOISIER

Let's all go to the Château—we'll calm all these alarms a bit.

CURTAIN

THE SCHOOL FOR LOVERS
BY ALAIN-RENÉ LESAGE

CAST OF CHARACTERS

FRISTON, an enchanter

PIERROT, his valet

LEANDRE

ISABELLE

OLIVETTE, her maid

HARLEQUIN, Leandre's valet

A TROUPE OF GOBLINS

THE PLAY

The action takes place on Friston's enchanted island. The stage represents an island decorated by the power of the enchanter, Friston.

FRISTON:

Ho, there, Pierrot!

You, who only came to this island today,

Tell me—does the abode seem beautiful?

PIERROT:

Very beautiful.

FRISTON:

I am the enchanter, Friston.

I begged you for my service, and as

I want to make a pretty lad of you,

I will instruct you in magic.

I will teach you the terrible science

Of dark secrets that make the day go pale.

PIERROT:

Instead, why not teach me,

If it's possible,

The art of avoiding love's darts.

FRISTON:

What! Pierrot's afraid of becoming amorous?

PIERROT:

Oh! My word,

That's an affair already determined.

As you made me cleave the air with you,

I saw, passing through this garden,

A brunette —

What a fine bearing!

How beautiful she seemed to me!

FRISTON:

Well?

PIERROT:

Well, I feel for her —

You understand me perfectly —

FRISTON:

The person who concerns you, my friend,

Is named Olivette.

She belongs to the beauty that I love,

She's the maid of Isabelle.

PIERROT:

Fine, fine. So much the better.

Since she's your mistress's chambermaid,

She's rightfully mine.

FRISTON:

No question.

PIERROT:

Hey, if you please,

What are these poor creatures

Doing in this deserted island?

FRISTON:

On that subject,

I have a confidence to make to you.

PIERROT:

I am disposed to give you an audience.

FRISTON:

Borne on an invisible chariot,

I passed through Florence one day.

PIERROT:

(interrupting him) It's a beautiful city,

That Florence. Continue.

FRISTON:

My heart, long at peace,

No longer thought of finding love.

PIERROT:

Oh, damn!

Cupid's a little wiseguy who intrudes everywhere.

FRISTON:

Allow me to speak, if you will.

PIERROT:

Continue, sir, continue.

FRISTON:

I observed the lovable Isabelle.

She was dreaming on a green lawn.

As soon as I was there for her —

PIERROT:

(sings) Love troubled your reason?

(speaking) Isn't it so? You became amorous, all at once, like me?

FRISTON:

Are you always going to interrupt me?

(singing) Far from rushing, like a passionate lover,

To declare my flames right away,

I wanted to know the depth

Of the sentiments in the beauty's heart.

I discovered that a faithful cavalier

Occupied her softest moments.

PIERROT:

Nice discovery, my word!

FRISTON:

Again?

PIERROT:

Continue, Mr. Enchanter, continue.

FRISTON:

And you, Mr. Pierrot, quit it.

You begin to make me impatient.

(singing) I decided to ravish Isabelle

From this rival who reigned in her heart.

PIERROT:

(sings) A poor lover is soon on the wing,

When for a rival he finds an enchanter.

FRISTON:

You don't intend to shut up, chatterbox?

PIERROT:

Go on, sir, I won't say anything more.

FRISTON:

Quickly, I formed a cloud.

I surrounded the lovers,

And to this peaceful island

I transported them in a moment.

PIERROT:

I guess indeed what you've done to the girl,

But what's become of the lad?

FRISTON:

In a magnificent palace,

Which I made expressly for them,

My magic art ceaselessly

Teaches them a thousand games.

FRISTON:

(aside) Right. I think he's mad.

FRISTON:

These lovers are always together,

With spirits devoted to me

That around them my order musters,

Making them observe this law.

PIERROT:

What, it's you who ordered

That they always be together?

FRISTON:

Assuredly.

PIERROT:

My mother was quite obliging.

Sir, you are even more so.

FRISTON:

Ignoramus!

(Singing) Learn that love deserts a heart

As soon as it sees itself at peace;

So, to make happiness distasteful,

It only has to be made easy.

PIERROT:

My word, let's sing. The more I will drink,

The more you will see me impaired.

FRISTON:

(laughing) Hey, dummy.

PIERROT:

(laughing, too) Hey, dupe!

(sings) By Jove!

You are really telling me a tall tale!

If —

FRISTON:

After two months, my rival

Must be really tired of Isabelle.

PIERROT:

Is your rival French?

FRISTON:

No. He's an Italian,

But even if he were a Spaniard,

He couldn't resist it.

PIERROT:

And tell me, sir,

Does Olivette also have a lover?

FRISTON:

Yes. Harlequin, Leandre's valet, is with her here.

PIERROT:

And they are together at all moments?

FRISTON:

Like their masters.

PIERROT:

Come on. All we'll get are the leftovers.

FRISTON:

Ah! Judge better of Isabelle and Olivette!

They are virtuous.

PIERROT:

Still, that's no fault of yours.

FRISTON:

Go. I guarantee you the master and

The valet are disgusted with their mistresses.

I tell you the remedy is infallible.

(singing) Yes, I protest:

This remedy will work.

PIERROT:

Oh! I see the rest,

The success it will have.

FRISTON:

It's already working.

I notice Leandre and Harlequin are

Separating a bit from their beauties.

(striking Pierrot with his ring)

Let's be invisible to hear what they are saying.

HARLEQUIN:

(entering) Lovers who you pity,

You are too happy.

LEANDRE:

Hey, about what, my friend,

Would you pity yourself?

HARLEQUIN:

About what?

To always see Olivette,

And to see her without anyone

To be found to tell about it.

I'd just as well like to be her husband.

LEANDRE:

There's nothing in this likable retreat,

That doesn't poison your fate.

Exquisite wines and admirable cheer.

HARLEQUIN:

Oh! Without it I would die!

LEANDRE:

All pleasures are gathered for us here

Where can you find finer concerts?

HARLEQUIN:

Yes, but sir,

Our games always resemble

Certain recent operas.

(speaking) There's nobody here.

You compose the box, Isabelle and you.

Olivette the balcony, me, the pit:

Brilliant assembly!

LEANDRE:

What do you want?

We have succumbed to the power of an enchanter.

HARLEQUIN:

To the devil with dull enchanters,

Him, his island, and all his goblins.

He joins

Lovers like rabbits

In this calm abode,

We yawn, we get bored, we fall asleep.

LEANDRE:

I know that only too well.

HARLEQUIN:

There's no pleasure in quietly possessing a heart:

Long live complications!

What joy to have to force the trenches of a stern mother,

To win the road blocked by an interesting maid servant,

Or to take the impossible from a jealous husband!

LEANDRE:

It's only too true.

HARLEQUIN:

I regret the time Olivette's aunt

Made me enraged by her vigilance.

LEANDRE:

I wish Isabelle's tutor was crossing my amorous plans.

I must confess, Harlequin, my untroubled happiness begins to tire me.

HARLEQUIN:

There's no way of getting out of it, sir.

LEANDRE:

I notice Isabelle and Olivette in this alley.

Let's avoid them.

HARLEQUIN:

Yes. We'll procure ourselves that pleasure.

LEANDRE:

What pain to love without constraint.

To be able to form your vows without fear.

HARLEQUIN:

No. Without the rigors and the alarms,

Love's pleasure has no charms.

(Leandre and Harlequin withdraw.)

FRISTON:

Well, this business

Is on its way, Pierrot.

PIERROT:

Your thesis is plain,

I'm just a dummy.

From now on I hope

To be welcomed here

FRISTON:

We must also learn

The feelings of our beauties.

(sighing)

Alas, perhaps they're

More faithful to their lovers.

(speaking) Still, that wouldn't be natural. They're approaching.

Let's listen to them.

(Isabelle appears sad. Olivette dances and wants to get her mistress to dance as well.)

OLIVETTE:

(dragging Isabelle)

Let's dance the new cotillion.

Bestir yourself, beauty,

Bestir yourself, then.

ISABELLE:

Leave me alone. What extravagance!

Why these transports and this excitement?

OLIVETTE:

Stop being uneasy.

In this happy moment,

Imitate Olivette,

And let's dance together.

Let's be gay,

With a gay air.

ISABELLE:

Olivette, quit it. Joy bores me.

OLIVETTE:

Joy bores you! Go rejoin Leandre.

(singing) Eh, leave me alone, cruel woman,

To play in this garden.

Oh the novel sweetness

To be without Harlequin.

Let's be gay

With a gay air.

(speaking) We were walking all together in the same alley the first day.

ISABELLE:

Yes.

OLIVETTE:

We love to walk separately at this time.

ISABELLE:

It is true. What a change, my dear Olivette!

The first days, I pardon to the enchanter for having kidnapped me.

OLIVETTE:

And me, too. I even laughed when I thought of the manner

Which he employed with us to detach us from our

lovers.

ISABELLE:

We regarded him like a madman.

OLIVETTE:

Hey, the old rogue! How well he knew women.

ISABELLE:

Oh, that I were still under the strict empire of my tutor.

OLIVETTE:

Oh, why am I not still scolded and insulted by my aunt!

Ah! My aunt!

Ah! My aunt!

When I fumed against you

I was only an ignoramus!

Ah, my aunt!

Ah, my aunt!

ISABELLE:

What would Harlequin say if he heard you?

(singing) Alas! If this faithful lover

Were instructed in his misfortune

He would go hang himself with sorrow!

OLIVETTE:

I will pay for the rope.

ISABELLE:

You are really generous! As for me, I apprehend that

Leandre is noticing my change; I know him, he'll die of it.

PIERROT:

(low to Friston) Make me visible, and I am going to

Announce to them the new feast you intend to give them.

(Friston gives him a tap with his ring and withdraws. Pierrot heads towards Olivette, dancing and singing aside.)

PIERROT:

Holding my dignity,

Let's go to these children,

These wenches, my word,

Are tempting enough.

And bing, bang, bing,

Lisa, the Soubrette,

And boom, bam, boom,

Lisette the Lison.

OLIVETTE:

Oh, oh, now there's the most funny of all

The disguised spirits we've seen up to now.

PIERROT:

(aside, making himself agreeable) They are ogling me.

(dancing and singing)

And bing, bang, bing.

Lisette the Soubrette

And bing, bam, boom

Lisette the Lison.

(speaking)

Let's pay them a well-turned compliment. (bows to them)

Ladies. I kiss your hands. Milord the enchanter,

My master, wants to regale you. (singing)

Prepare yourself for the latest party.

ISABELLE:

(with a sad air) What? Yet another party!

OLIVETTE:

(yawning) Yet another party!—

PIERROT:

Yes, yet another party. You aren't there!

(singing) The enchanter who brought you

Prepared for you a hundred years.

You and your lovers will be

Always together during this time.

The enchanter who brought you

Prepared for you a hundred years.

OLIVETTE:

May the devil take him with his parties!

PIERROT:

Oh! This is going to be fun!

(singing)

The song about it will be magnificent.

OLIVETTE:

What, your eternal music

Intends through its afflicting air

To eternalize our migraines?

The opera gives quarter to folks

At least three times a week.

PIERROT:

Through a new enchantment,

Made expressly to please you,

You are going to see in a bowl

Some bourgeois of Cythera.

Of their concerts I hear the sound

The folderol,

The folderol.

(to Olivette, pointing to Harlequin who approaches)

And there comes your cherished lover.

OLIVETTE:

Biribiri,

In the fashion of Barbary,

Mon ami.

(Leandre and Harlequin arrive. They don't have the disconcerted air of their mistresses.)

LEANDRE:

(low to Harlequin) Isabelle has penetrated my inconstancy.

She appears overwhelmed with sorrow.

HARLEQUIN:

(low to Leandre) Olivette is pouting, too.

ISABELLE:

(low to Olivette) Leandre's observing my change.

His despair is bursting out.

OLIVETTE:

(low to Isabelle) Harlequin is reading

In the depths of my heart.

PIERROT:

I believe that you respect me;

It seems to me you constrain yourself.

Let's go, children, prattle,

Always sit together.

Now that you have everything,

They'd take you for married couples.

(He makes Leandre sit by Isabelle on a bench, and Harlequin with Olivette on another. The four lovers perform a lazzi and imperceptibly distance themselves from each other, and give off signs of boredom. Hardly have they been seated, when a vessel appears with goblins disguised as cupids who descend to the tunes of different instruments. They are accompanied by other spirits in the form of inhabitants of Cythera.)

AN INHABITANT OF CYTHERA:

Fie on the most beautiful chain,

If one is choked too much by it.

You've got to become unfaithful,

Love demands liberty.

CHORUS OF SPIRITS:

Fie on the most beautiful chain,

If one is choked too much by it.

You've got to become unfaithful,

Love demands liberty.

(The spirits form a dance after which they sing the following.)

AN INHABITANT OF CYTHERA:

The lover pressed by a too-warm flame

Thinks that perfect happiness

Is always to see his mistress.

With nothing troubling his ardor,

That's the error of a youthful spirit;

In Cythera they laugh at it.

CHORUS:

That's the error of a youthful spirit.

In Cythera they laugh at it.

A FEMALE INHABITANT OF CYTHERA:

With a young girl, the aged mother

Believes by making the guard tight

To prevent her going to Cythera

After the voyage has already been made.

That's the error of an aged spirit;

In Cythera they laugh at it.

CHORUS:

That's the error of an aged spirit;

In Cythera they laugh at it.

PIERROT:

The husband who now sees

A werewolf in his wife,

Counts on her diabolic virtue

Although he doesn't make a penny.

He's nonetheless a cuckold;

In Cythera they laugh at him.

(After they sing these songs, the actors leave, except for Pierrot and the lovers.)

HARLEQUIN:

A dumb brunette,

Who smiles at any old thing,

Thinks every smirk of hers

Is pretty as can be.

In her bedroom they applaud it,

On the stairway they laugh at it.

OLIVETTE:

(rising and looking at Harlequin with a disdainful air)

The most tiresome black man,

Always ready to make a bad joke,

Thinks to divert with his sallies

A woman he's causing to yawn.

With a look they applaud him,

Behind the fan she laughs at him.

HARLEQUIN:

(to Olivette) I don't know this black man.

OLIVETTE:

And the dumb brunette, do you know her, Mr. Turk?

(Sings) Now, there's my jesting booby. (repeat)

HARLEQUIN:

So then I'm a black man? (repeat)

Ah! You're looking for a fight!

If I displease you, beauty,

Let's break up.

OLIVETTE:

Let's break up.

HARLEQUIN:

Shake!

OLIVETTE:

And bake!

TOGETHER:

Let's break up.

HARLEQUIN:

I am light as a balloon.

OLIVETTE:

As for me, I'm like a feather.

LEANDRE:

(rising and laughing) Ah! By Jove, how crazy Olivette is!

ISABELLE:

(rising in wrath) Harlequin is insolent!

(Leandre strikes Olivette on the shoulder, who performs a lazzi of hunting a bird, saying—)

OLIVETTE:

Chou, chou.

LEANDRE:

What are you doing?

OLIVETTE:

(singing) It's my poor love flying away.

HARLEQUIN:

Mine wasn't so slow.

ISABELLE:

(to Leandre, who laughs)

What, you're laughing at this idle talk,

You support this inconstant!

HARLEQUIN:

(aside) Beauty, he guards you too much.

Goodbye, all good things come to an end.

LEANDRE:

(affecting scorn) I can see, flighty Isabelle,

You want to break a sweet chain.

OLIVETTE:

(to Leandre) Sir, do you count for nothing,

Being faithful for two months?

ISABELLE:

Ah! It is over! I must avenge myself!

Perfidious lover, my flames are outraged.

To reproach me, for no reason, that I'm changeable,

Alas, that tells me too plainly, you are changing.

HARLEQUIN (looking maliciously at Olivette and taking a sad tone)

Already, from this change,

Regrets cling to us.

OLIVETTE:

(reciprocating) Assuredly, we are going

To die at this moment

(in a sneering tone) Go see if they're coming, Jack.

HARLEQUIN:

(imitating her) Go see if they're coming.

(Friston appears.)

FRISTON:

What's all this brouhaha?

OLIVETTE:

(with emotion) Don't come to reconcile us.

FRISTON:

What's it all about?

HARLEQUIN:

No, I beg you.

Plague! You know better than that.

LEANDRE:

(to Friston) Mercy, release me from these chains.

ISABELLE:

Let me leave this island.

OLIVETTE:

(pointing to Leandre and Harlequin)

Far from these odious objects,

Place us in some town.

HARLEQUIN:

(pointing to Isabelle and Olivette)

So as not to see these she-monkeys any more,

I'm ready to go to Canada.

FRISTON:

You must give Isabelle to me.

LEANDRE:

I consent to it; be her spouse.

PIERROT:

(to Harlequin, pointing to Olivette)

And you, renounce this beauty.

HARLEQUIN:

Oh! Willingly, she is yours.

PIERROT:

This fine kid knows how to touch my soul.

HARLEQUIN:

What do I care? Love her.

PIERROT:

At dawn I intend to make her my wife.

HARLEQUIN:

Would she were already!

PIERROT:

I am charmed by his gracious affectations.

HARLEQUIN:

I've had it up to here,

As for me,

I've had it up to here.

FRISTON:

(to Isabelle) And you, without reluctance

Are you leaving your lover?

You keep silent.

OLIVETTE:

So as to be blunt about it,

Provide us a way,

To leave instantly.

And above all, whatever it costs,

We will pay you cash.

PIERROT:

Right, right. The cow is ours.

(to Olivette) My pretty, would you

Marry Pierrot?

OLIVETTE:

I take you in a heartbeat.

PIERROT:

(offering his hand) Put it there, my sweet.

OLIVETTE:

Yes, to get out of this hell-house,

I'd marry the devil.

Yo-ho,

I'd marry the devil.

PIERROT:

I ask of you the mark of preference.

OLIVETTE:

Oh! You deserve it completely!

ISABELLE:

(to Friston) Lord, I give you my hand,

Rescue me from slavery.

OLIVETTE:

I would like to be,

Tomorrow, sweetly married.

(speaking) But, gentlemen, it's a condition

That you don't keep us shut in with you.

That would be even worse.

FRISTON:

No. You will be mistresses of your actions.

PIERROT:

As soon as you will be our wives,

You will become two great ladies.

We will see you very rarely.

You will have gallants galore.

OLIVETTE:

The role truly flatters us.

We will know how to defend ourselves.

LEANDRE:

(to Friston) Mercy, Mr. Enchanter,

Let's get this over with.

FRISTON:

It couldn't go better,

Let's end the adventure.

ISABELLE:

We are leaving these parts forever.

LEANDRE:

Make it a double-sized carriage.

HARLEQUIN:

Distance us from our Cloris,

Whose weight is killing us.

And transport us to Paris.

OLIVETTE:

In that case, take us to Rome.

CURTAIN

ABOUT THE EDITOR

Frank J. Morlock has written and translated many plays since retiring from the legal profession in 1992. His translations have also appeared on Project Gutenberg, the Alexandre Dumas Père web page, Literature in the Age of Napoléon, Infinite Artistries.com, and Munsey's (formerly Blackmask). In 2006 he received an award from the North American Jules Verne Society for his translations of Verne's plays. He lives and works in México.